On the Take

Stolen Asset Recovery (StAR) Series

StAR—the Stolen Asset Recovery Initiative—is a partnership between the World Bank Group and the United Nations Office on Drugs and Crime (UNODC) that supports international efforts to end safe havens for corrupt funds. StAR works with developing countries and financial centers to prevent the laundering of the proceeds of corruption and to facilitate more systematic and timely return of stolen assets.

The Stolen Asset Recovery (StAR) Series supports the efforts of StAR and UNODC by providing practitioners with knowledge and policy tools that consolidate international good practice and wide-ranging practical experience on cutting edge issues related to anticorruption and asset recovery efforts. For more information, visit www.worldbank .org/star.

Titles in the Stolen Asset Recovery (StAR) Series

Stolen Asset Recovery: A Good Practices Guide for Non-Conviction Based Asset Forfeiture (2009) by Theodore S. Greenberg, Linda M. Samuel, Wingate Grant, and Larissa Gray

Politically Exposed Persons: Preventive Measures for the Banking Sector (2010) by Theodore S. Greenberg, Larissa Gray, Delphine Schantz, Carolin Gardner, and Michael Latham

Asset Recovery Handbook: A Guide for Practitioners (2011) by Jean-Pierre Brun, Larissa Gray, Clive Scott, and Kevin Stephenson

Barriers to Asset Recovery: An Analysis of the Key Barriers and Recommendations for Action (2011) by Kevin Stephenson, Larissa Gray, and Ric Power

The Puppet Masters: How the Corrupt Use Legal Structures to Hide Stolen Assets and What to Do About It (2011) by Emile van der Does de Willebois, J.C. Sharman, Robert Harrison, Ji Won Park, and Emily Halter

Public Office, Private Interests: Accountability through Income and Asset Disclosure (2012)

On the Take: Criminalizing Illicit Enrichment to Fight Corruption (2012) by Lindy Muzila, Michelle Morales, Marianne Mathias, and Tammar Berger

On the Take

Criminalizing Illicit Enrichment to Fight Corruption

Lindy Muzila
Michelle Morales
Marianne Mathias
Tammar Berger

Stolen Asset Recovery Initiative

The World Bank • UNODC

ISBN (paper): 978-0-8213-9454-0
ISBN (electronic): 978-0-8213-9596-7
DOI: 10.1596/978-0-8213-9454-0

Cover photos: Shutterstock and photos.com
Cover design: Naylor Design

Library of Congress Cataloging-in-Publication Data
On the take : Criminalizing illicit enrichment to fight corruption / Lindy Muzila . . . [et al.].
     p. cm.
   Includes bibliographical references.
   ISBN 978-0-8213-9454-0 — ISBN 978-0-8213-9596-7 (electronic)
 1. Unjust enrichment (International law) I. Muzila, Lindy.
   K920.O5 2012
   345'.02323—dc23

                                                                              2012028809

Contents

Boxes

Figures

Tables

Acknowledgments

This study is the result of collaborative efforts from colleagues around the world. Their time and expertise enabled practitioners to impart their knowledge and experiences about the reality of the illicit enrichment offense in the jurisdictions that criminalize it.

This publication was written by Lindy Muzila (team leader, Stolen Asset Recovery Initiative [StAR]), Michelle Morales (StAR), Marianne Mathias (project consultant, StAR), and Tammar Berger (project consultant, StAR).

The authors are especially grateful to Adrian Fozzard (coordinator, StAR), Jean Pesme (coordinator, StAR), Dimitri Vlassis (chief of the Corruption and Economic Crime Branch, United Nations Office on Drugs and Crime [UNODC]), and Brigitte Strobel-Shaw (chief, Conference Support Section, Corruption and Economic Crime Branch, UNODC) for their ongoing support and guidance on this project.

The study benefited from the collaboration with the United Nations Office of the High Commissioner for Human Rights (OHCHR), which generously shared its time and experience under the guidance of Ayuush Bat-Erdene (chief, Right to Development Section, OHCHR), assisted by Basil Fernando (project consultant, OHCHR).

During the course of this study, valuable contributions that helped to shape the study were received from Matthew Adler (project consultant, United States), Yassine Allam (Tunisia), Noemie Apollon (project consultant, Canada), Silvina Coarsi (project consultant, Argentina), Chantal Herberstein (Austria), Rutherford Hubbard (United States), Guillermo Jorge (project consultant, Argentina), Eva Melis (Germany), Hari Mulukutla (project consultant, United States), Yousef Nasrallah (project consultant), and Chiara Redini (Italy).

The team is also grateful to all the authorities who took the time to fill out the questionnaire regarding the implementation of illicit enrichment in their jurisdictions. Special thanks go, in particular, to the authorities in Argentina; Hong Kong SAR, China; India; and Pakistan, who provided extensive information on their illicit enrichment frameworks, jurisprudence, and statistics.

As part of the drafting and consultation process for this document, a practitioners workshop was held in Washington, DC, during April 2011. The practitioners brought experience in conducting illicit enrichment investigations and prosecutions in both civil and common law jurisdictions. The workshop also allowed fruitful dialogue between practitioners and researchers. The participants were Ayuush Bat-Erdene (OHCHR), Bertrand de Speville (United Kingdom/Hong Kong SAR, China), Ghulam Farooq (Pakistan), Basil Fernando (project consultant, OHCHR), Augustin Flah (World Bank), Clara Garrido (Colombia), Guillermo Jorge (project consultant, Argentina), Pranvera Kirkbride (United States), Rick Messick (World Bank), Laura Pop (World Bank), Venkata Rama Sastry (India), and Balwinder Singh (India).

The team also benefited from many insightful comments during the peer review process. The peer reviewers were Oliver Stolpe (UNODC), Rick Messick (World Bank), Clara Garrido (Colombia), Agustin Flah (World Bank), Roberta Solis Ribeiro (Brazil Office of the Comptroller General), Ayuush Bat-Erdene (OHCHR), Basil Fernando (consultant, OHCHR), Ted Greenberg (consultant, StAR), Panagiotis Papadimitriou (UNODC), Lisa Bhansali (World Bank), Tim Steele (StAR), and Jacinta Oduor (StAR).

A special thanks also to Eli Bielasiak for arranging the logistics of the workshop in Washington, DC, as well as for his continued support in this project.

Lindy Muzila
Task Team Leader
StAR

Abbreviations

ANI	National Integrity Agency, Romania
AML	anti-money-laundering
AUCPCC	African Union Convention on Preventing and Combating Corruption
ECOWAS	Economic Community of West African States
FATF	Financial Access Task Force
FIU	financial intelligence unit
GDP	gross domestic product
IACAC	Inter-American Convention against Corruption
ICCPR	International Covenant on Civil and Political Rights
INTERPOL	International Criminal Police Organization
MLA	mutual legal assistance
NAB	National Accountability Bureau
NGO	nongovernmental organization
OHCHR	Office of the High Commissioner for Human Rights
POCA	Proceeds of Crime Act
SAR	Special Administrative Region
StAR	Stolen Asset Recovery Initiative
STR	suspicious transaction report
UNCAC	United Nations Convention against Corruption

Executive Summary

Illicit enrichment is criminalized under Article 20 of the United Nations Convention against Corruption (UNCAC), which defines it as the "significant increase in the assets of a public official that he or she cannot reasonably explain in relation to his or her lawful income." Illicit enrichment is also prescribed as an offense in the Inter-American Convention against Corruption (IACAC) and the African Union Convention on Preventing and Combating Corruption (AUCPCC) under comparable definitions. Despite such broad international recognition, the criminalization of illicit enrichment is not universally accepted as an anticorruption measure. Instead, it continues to generate extensive debate and controversy.

Against this background and based on country experience, this study aims to analyze how the criminalization of illicit enrichment works and to shed light on its contributions to the fight against corruption and the recovery of stolen assets. This study does not delve deeply into the theoretical debates around illicit enrichment, but instead analyzes practice, case law, and the literature to add new perspective to the ongoing discussions.

This study does not seek to recommend or oppose the adoption of particular illicit enrichment provisions. Rather, it aims to assist jurisdictions that are considering such steps by highlighting key questions that might arise during implementation, including how states define and enforce the offense. Similarly, this study does not endorse or criticize any practice carried out by states in implementing the criminalization of illicit enrichment. Ultimately, it seeks to provide useful information for policy makers and practitioners as well as for upcoming discussions of the Conference of State Parties of the UNCAC and its working groups.

This study found that 44 jurisdictions have criminalized illicit enrichment, most of them in developing countries. Several jurisdictions that prosecute illicit enrichment and that were contacted during the course of this study perceive it as a valuable complement to the traditional toolkit for combating corruption. However, the statistical information collected for this study indicates that only a limited number of these jurisdictions regularly investigate or prosecute the offense. Several elements of the illicit enrichment offense are common to the jurisdictions that prosecute it. Those elements are persons of interest, period of interest, significant increase in assets, intent, and absence of justification.

One critical issue subject to ongoing debate relates to the compatibility of illicit enrichment with human rights principles and related concerns regarding the perceived reversal of the burden of proof. Experience in several jurisdictions that have overcome these challenges shows that illicit enrichment offenses can be defined and implemented in a manner that fully respects the rights of the accused.

Considered in a broader context, there is the question of whether the public interest in the fight against corruption justifies the criminalization of illicit enrichment, an offense that contains some form of presumption. In this respect, several practices as well as jurisprudence have emerged that reconcile such presumptions with the respect for and protection of human rights. For instance, the jurisprudence of the European Court of Human Rights clearly delineates that the presumption of innocence does not prevent legislatures from creating criminal offenses containing a presumption by law as long as the principles of rationality and proportionality are duly respected. Similarly, many countries that do not criminalize illicit enrichment have enacted other offenses that do reverse the burden of proof to some extent. These related presumptions indicate that measures to shift the burden of proof can be considered as valid and legitimate tools for combating crime when justified by the public interest. Therefore, parallels may be drawn between these presumptions and the principle of illicit enrichment.

Apart from substantive aspects of the offense, research conducted for this study revealed that the design and implementation of government structures are critical to ensure full respect of Article 2 of the International Covenant on Civil and Political Rights (ICCPR). The status and existence of legislative, administrative, and judicial measures for the implementation of these rights must be considered from the point of view of the elimination of corruption. Of particular relevance is whether institutions involved in the investigation, prosecution, and adjudication of illicit enrichment are properly monitored, accountable, resourced, and trained so that they are in a position to implement the obligations taken under the ICCPR and to pursue corrupt money effectively and fairly. Any illicit enrichment legislation should be tailored to suit the particular needs and concerns of the country, specifically with regard to legislative, administrative, and judicial measures, including the role and limits of the prosecution.

Dual criminality remains a hurdle in international cooperation involving illicit enrichment. This is a challenge facing many of the countries prosecuting this offense, particularly when efforts are not made, before seeking assistance, to verify that the conduct underlying the request constitutes an offense in the requested jurisdiction. Several jurisdictions have publicly indicated their willingness to provide mutual legal assistance, even if they have not criminalized illicit enrichment themselves, provided that the conduct in question can be classified as an offense within their legal system. Translating such openness into actual information sharing requires a strong capacity to deconstruct the criminal conduct and to ensure the quality of the request for mutual legal assistance accordingly.

In all jurisdictions reviewed, the illicit enrichment law addresses the recovery of the assets illicitly acquired. However, there remains an absence of solid statistical data with which to establish whether such laws have actually contributed to the recovery of assets. The available evidence is mixed, and the underlying reasons for the mixed results are difficult to determine. One possibility is that convictions for illicit enrichment lead to penalties other than confiscation. These examples confirm that illicit enrichment laws can be useful in asset recovery, but there is still a long way to go before they are used systematically.

In sum, the limited experience available demonstrates that illicit enrichment can be a useful anticorruption and asset recovery tool that is implemented in full respect of human rights. It is hoped that the experiences documented in this study will promote greater understanding of how illicit enrichment works in practice. Further work may be carried out on institutional issues relating to investigations, prosecutions, and the judiciary as important agencies in the prosecution of illicit enrichment and the protection of the rule of law. Ultimately, more countries will gain experience in this arena and more statistics and information will become available. In the meantime, it is hoped that this study will provide the foundation for further examination of how illicit enrichment frameworks could help countries to facilitate the recovery of corruption proceeds.

Introduction: Purpose of the Study

In November 2009, the third session of the Conference of State Parties of the United Nations Convention against Corruption (UNCAC) adopted Resolution 3/3, which urged "further study and analysis of, inter alia, the results of asset recovery actions and, where appropriate, how legal presumptions, measures to shift the burden of proof, and the examination of illicit enrichment frameworks could facilitate the recovery of corruption proceeds."[1] The resolution responded to interest expressed by many state parties in how different jurisdictions have implemented the criminalization of illicit enrichment.

This study responds to the call for such analysis. Its objectives are, first, to promote a broader understanding of the offense of illicit enrichment, its application, benefits, and the challenges it poses and, second, based on country experience, to identify key issues that jurisdictions should consider when developing an institutional and legal regime for criminalizing illicit enrichment.

In particular, the study looks at whether the criminalization of illicit enrichment has facilitated the recovery of assets by national authorities and examines the related challenges they have experienced in this respect. The study also addresses key issues identified by these authorities, which include putting in place effective institutional and legislative regimes for criminalizing, identifying, and prosecuting illicit enrichment with the help of mutual legal assistance.

Further, this publication examines how the concept of illicit enrichment is applied in those jurisdictions currently implementing and enforcing the offense, particularly in view of expressed and documented concerns. It describes risks posed to the fairness of the trial process if the accused is required to provide a "reasonable explanation" of his assets. Building on existing legislation and case law, the study identifies the safeguards used by states and related measures intended to ensure a balanced and fair trial. In order to contextualize the debate with regard to the burden of proof, the study also outlines measures that some jurisdictions have used instead of the concept of illicit enrichment, such as reversing some of the burden of proof in efforts to confiscate the proceeds of crime and to prosecute crimes related to the abuse of positions of trust.[2]

---

1. UNCAC, Resolution 3/3, para. 13.
2. See UNCAC, Article 31(8), which provides that state parties may wish to consider shifting the burden of proof to the accused, who then must show that proceeds were obtained from legitimate sources.

This review does not seek to rank one approach over another nor single out any jurisdiction. Instead, by providing an overview of different approaches, it seeks to identify lessons learned, to highlight the challenges of using the criminalization of illicit enrichment as a framework for anticorruption and asset recovery efforts, and to inform the debate surrounding illicit enrichment.

Methodology

This study builds on published research on the criminalization of illicit enrichment. Most of this literature focuses on constitutional and human rights implications of the offense. The practical issues related to the investigation and prosecution of illicit enrichment have received scant attention, save in a few instances. Given the focus of the World Bank's Stolen Asset Recovery Initiative (StAR) on operational issues related to asset recovery, as well as the objective of adding value to ongoing discussions, the study focuses primarily on learning from the experiences of states that have implemented a legal framework for prosecuting illicit enrichment.

This study also draws upon a review of the records of negotiations for the UNCAC, the drafting decisions of the key international conventions, and existing jurisprudence on illicit enrichment. An extensive search was conducted to identify jurisdictions that have legislation criminalizing illicit enrichment. The review draws extensively on the legal library of the United Nations Office on Drugs and Crime, a parallel project supported by StAR that was launched in the second half of 2011. It also surveyed 45 national authorities, receiving 30 responses. The questionnaire is presented as appendix C to this study.

Appendix A lists the jurisdictions where, in the view of the team, illicit enrichment has been criminalized. Without endorsing any particular definition of "criminalization," in order to work with a distinct or more clearly defined standard, the team focused on countries that criminalize illicit enrichment by imposing the possibility of prison sanctions. Some provisions that are very similar to illicit enrichment were not included in appendix A. Implementation of these provisions was not subjected to an in-depth analysis, but is discussed where relevant. Some of these jurisdictions, such as Romania, have illicit enrichment provisions in their legal systems, but the related sanctions are not criminal in nature.[3] Brazil, for example, has adopted illicit enrichment as an act of administrative misconduct.[4] Burundi does not include the illicit enrichment provision, as it is considered unenforceable due to difficulties in its phrasing and the absence of

---

3. In Sudan, the Unlawful and Suspicious Enrichment (Combating) Act of 1989, Section 7, defines the crime of "suspicious enrichment" as "every such property, as may vest into any person, and he cannot explain any lawful aspect for acquiring the same." If the accused is convicted, the court may confiscate the property.

4. Law no. 8429 of 2 June 1992, Article 9, Section VII, defines illicit enrichment as "to secure for oneself or a third party, in the performance of a public office, position, post, or function, assets of any nature, the total value of which is disproportionate to the public official's past or present declared income or earnings." Brazil is considering criminalizing illicit enrichment by adding penal sanctions to the current

key elements.[5] Other countries have enacted provisions, which, although very similar to illicit enrichment, are not limited to the key elements. For example, some provisions require the prosecution to prove an additional element that is linked to particular wrongdoing or conduct. In Burkina Faso, the applicable provision requires the demonstration of "an unlawful action or misconduct from the public official"[6] through the use of money, property, title, document, object, or material belonging to the state.[7] Similarly, in Cyprus, the provision refers to a public official's acquisition of a property or benefit "by abuse or taking advantage of his/her office or capacity";[8] while in Jordan, the provision requires that the enrichment be on account of the public official "investing his/her position or capacity."[9] Because a "pure" illicit enrichment offense is only based on the unexplained increase in the assets of a public official, these provisions go a step further, requiring the prosecution to demonstrate a link between the unlawful action and the unexplained increase.

During the course of this study, a meeting was convened of practitioners from some civil and common law countries with prior experience prosecuting illicit enrichment cases in their jurisdictions. The experts were invited not only to comment on the draft, but also to provide substantive contributions based on their own experiences. Representatives of the Office of the High Commissioner for Human Rights (OHCHR) also attended the meeting and provided extremely valuable views on the constitutional and human rights aspects of the illicit enrichment offense.

---

administrative ones. A draft law has been pending in Congress since 2005 and was presented again for adoption in May 2011.

5. The Burundi Penal Code, Law 1/12 of 18 April 2006, Article 438, states, "Est punie d'une servitude pénale de trois ans à cinq ans et d'une amende portée du simple jusqu'au double de la valeur du bien, toute personne dépositaire de l'autorité publique, chargée d'une mission de service public ou investie d'un mandat public électif, dont l'origine illicite a été établie par une décision judiciaire." This provision does not refer to an unjustified increase in wealth.

6. The Burkina Faso Penal Code, Article 160, states, "Toute personne qui se sera enrichie en se servant de denier, matériel, titre, acte, objet, effet, ou tout autre moyen appartenant à l'etat sera puni selon le montant de l'enrichissement des peines prévues à l'article 154 ci-dessus."

7. Jurisprudence demonstrates that the Burkina Faso courts look at the circumstances of the conduct leading to the increase in assets, meaning that the prosecution has an additional burden of linking the conduct to the increase, see C. Cass, ch. crim, 23.12.2004; C. Cass, ch. crim 27.10.2005; C. Cass, ch. crim, 03.11.2006.

8. In Cyprus, under the Illicit Acquisition of Property Benefits by State Officials and Public Officers Law no. 51(I) of 2004, the offense of illicit enrichment is the acquisition of a "property benefit" by a state official or public officer by means of abuse or taking advantage of his or her office or capacity, in which the benefit goes directly or indirectly to himself or herself or to a member of his or her family or a relative up to the third degree of kindred. For the purposes of this law, "property benefit" means any kind of movable or immovable property, including money or business profit, shares, securities, bank deposits, and any kind of values. The offense carries a sentence of imprisonment up to seven years, a fine up to €42,715.00, or both. Furthermore, the court has power to order, in addition, confiscation of the illicitly acquired property or benefit.

9. In Jordan, the 2006 Income and Asset Disclosure Law no. 54, Article 6, states, "It shall be regarded as an illicit enrichment any property, movable or immovable, interest, right to an interest, gained by any person subject to this law, for him/herself or others, because of investing his/her position or capacity; and if there is a sudden increase in his/her property or his/her minor children's property after assuming such position or capacity that is not commensurate with his/her resources; and if s/he fails to demonstrate a legitimate source of such increase, it shall be regarded as resulting from investing his position or capacity."

How to Use This Study

Policy makers—senior officials, technical staff, and legislators of government agencies and international organizations working in corruption-related fields—are the primary audience for this study. StAR offers the study in the hopes that it will assist decision makers in designing, implementing, or monitoring the work of agencies responsible for implementing the legal framework for the criminalization of illicit enrichment and in improving the confiscation and recovery of assets. In addressing this audience, the study seeks to cover the key legal concepts and issues with broad strokes rather than a minute analysis of the legal arguments.

While this study provides some legal analysis of the issues, it does not delve deeply into the legal intricacies. Instead, it seeks to identify the pertinent questions that arise when discussing the adoption of illicit enrichment legislation and to consider the advantages and disadvantages of such legislation. It also seeks to provide policy makers with the necessary tools to implement the law. A comprehensive bibliography is provided for those seeking to explore the legal arguments or analysis in greater detail.

While primarily designed to inform policy makers, the study may also be useful to prosecutors and other practitioners who implement illicit enrichment laws. References to case law will be useful in exploring the strategy to be adopted in a particular case, although care should be taken to analyze cases in the context of the particular circumstances of the jurisdictions that rendered them. Similarly, the cases and legislation referred to in this study are illustrative and should therefore be viewed as a starting point, not a comprehensive source.

In spite of several attempts to generate a quantitative analysis of how illicit enrichment prosecution can facilitate asset recovery, very little information was obtained from participating countries. Nevertheless, quantitative information was included, when available, to indicate the experiences of those jurisdictions that are effectively prosecuting illicit enrichment.

The findings documented in this study are based on the experiences of jurisdictions that have enacted illicit enrichment legislation. This study does not aim to take a final stance in recommending or opposing the adoption of such legislation as a tool for addressing corruption or recovering stolen assets. The issues surrounding illicit enrichment—and the impact of its criminalization on corruption—are too complex, diverse, and country specific to allow for a one-size-fits-all recommendation.

1. The Basis of Illicit Enrichment

By preventing corrupt officials from enjoying the benefits of their ill-gotten gains, the state seeks to remove the underlying motivation for corruption. As such, asset recovery, international cooperation, civil and criminal confiscation regimes, and related mechanisms for securing the return of the proceeds of corruption are increasingly important efforts of law enforcement. However, a significant obstacle to the return of the proceeds of corruption is the difficulty of prosecuting corruption, which at times requires evidence that proves to be elusive and calls for costly technical expertise that few countries can master. In terms of detection, the victims of these corrupt acts—the public—may be unaware that the crime is taking place, meaning that the corruption often goes unreported. Frequently, those with access to the information that would allow for the detection of the crime may be complicit. Moreover, those involved in the crime may use power and influence to intimidate witnesses and destroy any evidence of their crimes.

1.1 The Rationale for Criminalizing Illegal Enrichment

Often, the only tangible evidence that a crime has taken place is the money that changes hands between the corrupt official and his partner in crime, thus the enrichment of the corrupt official becomes the most visible manifestation of corruption. An offense such as bribery, which requires the demonstration of an offer by the corruptor or acceptance by the official, is difficult to prosecute in these circumstances. Similarly, once an offense has been established in a court of law, linking the proceeds to an offense for the purposes of recovering assets can often be a complex endeavor. Efforts to combat corruption are further challenged by the anonymity and fluidity with which assets can be moved, concealed, and transferred before effective means can be taken to seize, freeze, and return them to their rightful owners.

In response, some states have adopted the offense of illicit enrichment to strengthen their ability to fight corruption and recover assets. Based on the idea that unexplained wealth of a public official may, in fact, be visible proceeds of corruption, illicit enrichment was identified as a nonmandatory crime in Article 20 of the United Nations Convention against Corruption (UNCAC) and defined, *when committed intentionally*, as a "significant increase in the assets of a public official that he or she cannot reasonably explain in relation to his or her lawful income." Box 1.1 describes a recent case of illicit enrichment.

The *State v. Mzumar:* Malawi

The accused—a public officer in the Immigration Department at the time in question—was charged with three counts of possession of unexplained property, contrary to Section 32(2)(C) of the Malawian Corrupt Practices Act of 1995, for the following:

- Having possessed between 1 January and 21 December 2008, assets in the sum of about US$62,000 disproportionate to his known sources of income amounting to about US$3,000
- Having deposited US$14,000, which was reasonably suspected to have been corruptly acquired, into a bank account
- Having possession of an unexplained plot and house worth US$4,000.

In support of the prosecution's case, one witness testified on the amount of his salary, two witnesses from different banks testified on the number and amount of deposits he had made into his account, and another testified on the value of the house he had sold to the accused. Lastly, the investigator testified that she had initiated the investigation after receiving information that the accused was involved in smuggling foreigners into the country for a monetary fee. The only evidence in support of this suspicion was that the accused had made phone calls to Ethiopia, Kenya, and Somalia.

In his defense, the accused testified that the additional sums to his salary were due to an allowance from the government, a loan from his office, and a rice business he was running. In addition to his explanation, one witness testified on his behalf.

The court found that the prosecution had demonstrated the following beyond a reasonable doubt:

- The accused was a public officer.
- He had in his possession pecuniary resources that were disproportionate to his present or past official emoluments or other known sources of income.
- He had failed to give a reasonable explanation, and the explanations given did not meet the balance of probabilities standard required in the circumstances.

As a result, the accused was convicted on all counts and sentenced to a prison term of 12 years.

Source: Criminal Case no. 47 of 2010.
Note: At the time of reporting, this case had not yet exhausted the appeals process.

1.2 The Prosecution of Illicit Enrichment

The criminalization of "illicit enrichment," frequently referred to as "disproportionate wealth" or "inexplicable wealth," allows states to, among other things, prosecute corrupt officials and confiscate the proceeds of corruption on the basis that the unexplained wealth is evidence of corrupt conduct. The need to prove that such wealth is unexplained stands, but in such frameworks, there is no need to prove the *source* of the illegally acquired wealth by identifying and proving the underlying offenses, such as bribery, embezzlement, trading in influence, and abuse of functions. As a result, the effect may extend beyond corruption and allow states to confiscate the proceeds of other crimes. Illicit enrichment is similar to money laundering in that there is no need to prove an underlying offense, although the criminal origins of funds still need to be proven in the case of money laundering.

In order to attain a conviction of illicit enrichment, the prosecution must demonstrate that the official's enrichment cannot be justified from legitimate sources of income, raising the presumption that it is the proceeds of corruption. The public official may rebut this presumption by providing evidence of the legitimate origin of his wealth. Failure to rebut the presumption results in a conviction and the imposition of penalties. Some view the presumption of illicit enrichment as a partial reversal of the burden of proof and a relaxation of the presumption of innocence, considered fundamental principles of all legal systems. As such, some consider the illicit enrichment offense as a violation of the right against self-incrimination and other due process rights. Others consider it as fully compliant with human rights principles, given the existence of similar presumptions in criminal law and the general principle that no fundamental right is absolute.

More generally, some hold the view that, given the difficulty of proving corruption, it is in the public interest to require public officials to explain how they acquired their wealth. Following this logic, the criminalization of illicit enrichment is essentially rooted in the contractual and fiduciary responsibilities that a public official assumes on taking up his post. This explains why the public official is the primary subject of this offense. A court in Argentina has held that the state sets the conditions for admission to the public service, fixes remuneration, and establishes disciplinary law. The candidate who accepts the office or employment as a public official therefore implicitly accepts the regime unilaterally established by the state.[10] To the same extent, he also accepts to file an asset disclosure form on a regular basis. This requirement, which sometimes includes disclosure of his bank accounts, is a legal duty related only to his public functions.

1.3 Origins and Development of the Offense

In 1936, a state congressman in Argentina by the name of Rodolfo Corominas Segura was traveling by train from his home in Mendoza to Buenos Aires when he encountered a public official displaying the wealth he had accumulated since taking office, wealth that Corominas Segura felt could not possibly have come from a legitimate source. Inspired, Corominas Segura introduced a bill stating that the government would penalize "public officials who acquire wealth without being able to prove its legitimate

---

10. Joseph M. Pico and K.B.U., Cámara Nacional de Casación Penal (National Chamber of Criminal Appeals).

source." Although this bill never became law, similar bills were introduced in successive legislatures until 1964.

In India, illicit enrichment was initially enacted as an evidentiary measure, rather than as a crime. Section 5(3) of the Prevention of Corruption Act laid out an evidentiary rule permitting the prosecution to demonstrate the perpetration of enumerated corruption offenses (bribery, trading in influence, misappropriation of public property, and criminal conduct in the mischarge of duty, as laid out in Sections 5.1.a–5.1.d) by demonstrating that the accused (a) possessed assets disproportionate to his or her known income and (b) did not have a satisfactory explanation for them. This entirely new rule was met with controversy because, as interpreted, the prosecution did not need to produce evidence of a corrupt act in order to obtain a conviction. At the same time, Section 5(3) could not be grounds for a conviction in and of itself.

In 1964, as a result of amendments to existing legislation, Argentina and India became the first countries to criminalize illicit enrichment. In India, the statute defines illicit enrichment as the possession of resources "for which the public servant cannot satisfactorily account," while Argentina defines it as the failure "to justify the origin of any appreciable enrichment for himself or a third party."[11]

In the 20 years since illicit enrichment was criminalized in Argentina and India, similar provisions have been introduced in Brunei Darussalam, Colombia, Ecuador, the Arab Republic of Egypt, the Dominican Republic, Pakistan, and Senegal. By 1990, illicit enrichment had been criminalized in at least 10 countries, by 2000 in more than 20 countries, and by 2010 in more than 40 jurisdictions. Like India, some of these countries simply criminalized provisions that already existed under their law of evidence.

---

11. India Prevention of Corruption Act of 1988, Article 13 states, "Criminal misconduct by a public servant. (1) A public servant is said to commit the offense of criminal misconduct, ... if he or any person on his behalf is in possession or has, at any time during the period of his office, been in possession for which the public servant cannot satisfactorily account, of pecuniary resources or property disproportionate to his known sources of income. This offense is also punishable with a minimum imprisonment of one year, extendable up to seven years, and also with a fine."

Argentine Criminal Code of 1964, Article 268(2), states, "Any person who, when so demanded, fails to justify the origin of any appreciable enrichment for himself or a third party in order to hide it, obtained subsequent to assumption of a public office or employment, and for up to two years after having ceased his duties, shall be punished by imprisonment from two to six years, a fine of 50 percent to 100 percent of the value of the enrichment, and absolute perpetual disqualification. Enrichment will be presumed not only when the person's wealth has been increased with money, things, or goods, but also when his debts have been canceled or his obligations extinguished. The person interposed to dissimulate the enrichment shall be punished by the same penalty as the author of the crime."

Article 268(3) states, "Any person who, by reason of his position, is required by law to present a sworn statement of assets and maliciously fails to do so shall be punished by imprisonment from 15 days to two years and special perpetual disqualification. The offense is deemed committed when, after due notice of the obligation, the person obligated has not complied with those duties within the time limits established by the applicable law. Any person who maliciously falsifies or omits data required in those sworn statements by the applicable laws and regulations shall be liable to the same penalty." Translation from OAS (2009c); the original is available in appendix A.

For others, illicit enrichment was a new concept and a radical tool in their fight against corruption.

The incorporation of illicit enrichment into three international anticorruption conventions undoubtedly accelerated the adoption of the offense. Illicit enrichment was first included in the Inter-American Convention against Corruption (IACAC), adopted by the Organization of American States in 1996, then in the African Union Convention on Preventing and Combating Corruption (AUCPCC), approved in 2003, and finally in the UNCAC, also approved in 2003 and entered into force in 2005. At a regional level, illicit enrichment was also included in the Economic Community of West African States (ECOWAS) Protocol on the Fight against Corruption, adopted in December 2001 but not yet in force.[12]

The IACAC is the only convention where illicit enrichment is a mandatory offense. When they ratified the IACAC, both Canada and the United States expressed reservations regarding the criminalization of illicit enrichment, citing its incompatibility with constitutional and human rights principles, notably the presumption of innocence (see also OAS 2010a, 92–93). There was further controversy during the UNCAC negotiations, with some authorities arguing that the illicit enrichment provision should be dropped and others suggesting that it should be shifted to the chapter on prevention and provide for only administrative sanctions (see, respectively, UN General Assembly 2002a, para. 42; 2002b, 33, fn. 188). In the end, UNCAC adopted illicit enrichment as a nonmandatory criminal offense and required states to *consider* criminalizing illicit enrichment "subject to the requirements of their constitutions and the fundamental principles" of their legal systems. The AUCPCC followed a similar approach.

Today, illicit enrichment provisions can be found in most regions of the world, with the notable exceptions of North America and most of Western Europe. Among countries choosing not to criminalize illicit enrichment by public officials, many have enacted alternative means for tackling it, such as measures making it easier either to prosecute or to confiscate illicit proceeds. Such legal dispositions usually rely on provisions regarding organized crime, which can sometimes lower or partially reverse the burden of proof for the prosecution.

---

12. ECOWAS Protocol, Article 6(3)(a) states, "L'enrichissement illicite consistant en une augmentation significative du patrimoine d'un agent public qu'il ne peut raisonnablement justifier par rapport aux revenus perçus légitimement dans l'exercice de ses fonctions sera considéré comme un acte de corruption pour les besoins du présent protocole par ceux des etats parties qui l'ont instauré comme tel." The English translation reads, "A significant increase in the assets of a public official that he cannot reasonably explain in relation to his lawful earnings shall be considered an illicit enrichment and an act of corruption for the purposes of this protocol among those state parties for which it is a criminal offense."

2. Defining Illicit Enrichment

2.1 International and Domestic Definitions

Definitions of enrichment identify and describe the elements of the offense, which are a series of essential components that must be present in order for an accused to be found guilty. They are defined in legislation and through the court's interpretations in jurisprudence. The three examples presented in table 2.1 illustrate the variations in the definition of illicit enrichment in international conventions.

International conventions seek to harmonize the elements of the crime across states, but, as shown in table 2.1, differences still exist between the key relevant conventions. In addition, the debates during the negotiations of the United Nations Convention against Corruption (UNCAC) further highlighted differences in the national perspectives with regard to the appropriate formulation of such elements. These differences notwithstanding, there are greater similarities than differences among the national approaches adopted (table 2.2). As a result, the trend has been toward developing some common elements of illicit enrichment. These are discussed further in section 2.2.

At this stage, it is important to note that, within the UNCAC, slight differences in translations into the official United Nations languages can lead to differing approaches in dealing with the offense. For instance, in Article 20, the English phrase "establish a criminal offense" becomes "tipificar el delito" in Spanish, with no more reference to the criminal characteristics of the offense, and becomes "conférer le caractère d'infraction pénale"[13] in French, which covers a wide range of offenses, from minor infractions to criminal offenses. Although the purpose of this study is not to assess a country's compliance with UNCAC provisions, it is useful to bear these differences in mind when considering implementation of illicit enrichment.

Seeking to harmonize the definition of illicit enrichment is intended to ensure that the focus is placed on the underlying conduct, not the name of the offense. In this respect, while some provisions similar to illicit enrichment are linked to the failure to disclose assets or the misstatement of income and asset disclosures, those provisions are usually based on noncompliance with disclosure laws and, for our purposes, are not considered illicit enrichment. Accordingly, while income and asset disclosures may be used to provide evidence of illicit enrichment and are discussed in this context in subsequent chapters, offenses arising out of noncompliance with income and asset disclosures are not addressed in this study (see StAR 2012 for a discussion). Also, some provisions use the term "illicit enrichment" for an offense that is actually a classical corruption offense,

---

13. French Penal Code, Article 111-1, states, "Les infractions pénales sont classées, suivant leur gravité, en crimes, délits, et contraventions."

TABLE 2.1	Definitions of Illicit Enrichment in International Conventions	
United Nations Convention against Corruption (UNCAC), Article 20	Inter-American Convention against Corruption (IACAC), Article Ix	African Union Convention on Preventing and Combating Corruption (AUCPCC), Article 8
Subject to its constitution and the fundamental principles of its legal system, each state party shall consider adopting such legislative and other measures as may be necessary to establish as a criminal offense, when committed intentionally, illicit enrichment, that is, a significant increase in the assets of a public official that he or she cannot reasonably explain in relation to his or her lawful income.	Subject to its constitution and the fundamental principles of its legal system, each state party that has not yet done so shall take the necessary measures to establish under its laws as an offense a significant increase in the assets of a government official that he cannot reasonably explain in relation to his lawful earnings during the performance of his functions.	Subject to the provisions of their domestic law, state parties undertake to adopt necessary measures to establish under their laws an offense of illicit enrichment. "Illicit enrichment" means the significant increase in the assets of a public official or any other person which he or she cannot reasonably explain in relation to his or her income (Article 1, Definitions).

TABLE 2.2	Definitions of Illicit Enrichment in National Legislation	
Sierra Leone (Anti-Corruption Act 2008, Part IV)	Guyana (Integrity Commission Act 1998)	China (Criminal Law 1997, Article 395)
(1) Any person who, being or having been a public officer having unexplained wealth, (a) maintains a standard of living above that which is commensurate with his present or past official emoluments or (b) is in control of pecuniary resources or property disproportionate to his present or past official emoluments, unless he gives a satisfactory explanation to the court as to how he was able to	Where a person who is or was a person in public life, or any other person on his behalf, is found to be in possession of property or pecuniary resource disproportionate to the known sources of income of the first mentioned person, and that person fails to produce satisfactory evidence to prove that the possession of the property or pecuniary resource was acquired by lawful means,	Any state functionary whose property or expenditure obviously exceeds his lawful income, if the difference is enormous, may be ordered to explain the sources of his property. If he cannot prove that the sources are legitimate, the part that exceeds his lawful income shall be regarded as illegal gains, and he shall be sentenced to fixed-term imprisonment of not more than

(continued next page)

TABLE 2.2	Definitions of Illicit Enrichment in National Legislation (cont.)	
Sierra Leone (Anti-Corruption Act 2008, Part IV)	Guyana (Integrity Commission Act 1998)	China (Criminal Law 1997, Article 395)
maintain such a standard of living or how such pecuniary resources or property came under his control, commits an offense.	he shall be guilty of an offense and shall be liable, on summary conviction, to a fine and to imprisonment for a term of not less than six months nor more than three years.	five years or criminal detention, and the part of property that exceeds his lawful income shall be recovered.

requiring an unlawful action or misconduct from the public official, while a "pure" illicit enrichment offense is based only on the unexplained increase in the assets of a public official.

2.2 Elements of the Offense

Based on the definitions found in the UNCAC, AUCPCC, and IACAC, the offense of illicit enrichment has five key elements: persons of interest, period of interest, conduct of enrichment (that is, the significant increase in assets), intent (including awareness or knowledge), and the absence of justification.

2.2.1 Persons of Interest

Illicit enrichment specifically targets public officials. All three of the aforementioned international conventions and all of the national enrichment laws reviewed in the course of this study identify public officials as the persons of interest—the individuals who may be prosecuted for the crime. Two issues merit further consideration: first, the categories of public officials that are included as persons of interest and, second, whether the persons of interest should include a wider range of individuals beyond public officials.

There is a clear preference among states for including expansive definitions of public officials in both the conventions and national legislation. Article 2 of UNCAC defines "public official" as

(i) any person holding a legislative, executive, administrative, or judicial office of a state party, whether appointed or elected, whether permanent or temporary, whether paid or unpaid, irrespective of that person's seniority; (ii) any other person who performs a public function, including for a public agency or public enterprise, or provides a public service, as defined in the domestic law of the state party and as applied in the pertinent area of law of that state party; (iii) any other person defined as a public official in the domestic law of a state party.

Where national legislation criminalizing illicit enrichment and supporting jurisprudence defines a public official, the definitions are similarly broad, generally encompassing public servants, functionaries, or, as in Guyana, "a person in public life."

Some countries have expanded the definition to include a wider range of individuals who have access to public resources or act in the public interest. India, for instance, defines "public officials" as persons serving the public interest, whether or not they carry the title of "public servant" or are "appointed by the government," and does not specify outer limits to this definition. Bhutan includes not only public servants, but also "a person having served or serving under a nongovernmental organization or such other organization using public resources." This approach reflects a focus on the abuse of a position of trust in relation to public officials who enrich themselves at the public's expense.

While most states have enacted illicit enrichment legislation directed toward public officials, some have extended it to the private sector. In this regard, Colombia has established illicit enrichment committed by private individuals as a stand-alone offense.[14] Similarly, Pakistan applies the illicit enrichment provision to a "holder of public office or any other person." As a consequence of this broader definition, underlying offenses other than corruption may be easily covered in Pakistan. The applicability of illicit enrichment to private persons has been tested before Pakistan's courts. In the case of *Abdul Aziz Memon v. State*,[15] a question arose as to whether the illicit enrichment provisions were applicable to a private person who is no longer holding public office. The accused in that case was a former member of the National Assembly of Pakistan. He was charged with having assets beyond known sources of income and was arrested and charged, together with his wife, in whose name the assets were held. Both were convicted by the Accountability Court and sentenced to seven years imprisonment, and their assets were confiscated. However, some of the assets in question were acquired in the period during which the husband was not a member of the National Assembly. In their appeal before the High Court, the defense contended that the accused was not accountable for the years during which he was not a member of the National Assembly and thereby not a holder of public office. In upholding the conviction, the High Court held in this respect,

> Consequence to the above discussion, we are persuaded to agree with the contention of Mr. S. M. Zafar that the scope of NAB [National Accountability Bureau] ordinance is wider in terms and is applicable to all citizens of Pakistan and all persons including the holders of public offices. The result is that the appellants are accountable for acquiring the assets from the year 1985 till the year 1996, the period for which they were tried.

---

14. See Act no. 599 of 2000. Criminal Code, Title X, Crimes against the Economic Social Order, Chapter V, Article 327, provides for "the illicit enrichment, for private individuals." It holds accountable whoever directly or through another person obtains, for his own benefit or for the benefit of a third party, an unjustified increase in assets, when it is determined to have been derived, in one form or another, from criminal activities.

15. *Abdul Aziz Memon v. State*, 2003 YLR 617, concerning provisions of Section 9(a)(v) relating to assets beyond known sources.

Other countries have sought to include individuals who are family members of a public official and therefore may be considered as potential beneficiaries or accomplices involved in hiding the proceeds of corruption. In El Salvador and the Arab Republic of Egypt, for instance, the offense extends to the capital or income held by the spouse and minor children of a public official. In Paraguay, investigators should consider assets held by first- and second-degree bloodline relatives.[16] The AUCPCC extends the scope of illicit enrichment further still to include "any person." This may be understood as supporting the prosecution of individuals in the private sector who receive bribes as well as family members and associates of public officials who receive illicit payments.

In practice, some provisions are directed toward recovering assets held by those individuals, rather than targeting close relatives and associates for prosecution. In Brunei Darussalam, for example, the illicit enrichment provision extends to the property of "any person holding pecuniary resources or property in trust for or otherwise on behalf of the accused or [having] acquired such pecuniary resources or property as a gift or loan without adequate consideration from the accused" to have been under the control of the accused and liable to seizure.[17]

Where the intention is to focus on corruption in the public sector, the UNCAC definition of public official will generally be sufficient to achieve the objectives of the law.[18] This definition does not exclude action against family members or associates. The financial affairs of these individuals will generally be examined in an illicit enrichment investigation of a public official. This approach is consistent with international agreements, notably UNCAC, Article 52, and Financial Action Task Force (FATF), Recommendation 6, which require enhanced monitoring of the family and close associates of prominent public officials in their interaction with financial institutions.[19] Where

---

16. Paraguay, Law no. 2.523/04, Article 3.

17. Brunei Darussalam, Prevention of Corruption Act 1982, Article 12, Possession of Unexplained Property.

18. UNCAC, Article 2, defines "'public official' as (i) any person holding a legislative, executive, administrative, or judicial office of a state party, whether appointed or elected, whether permanent or temporary, whether paid or unpaid, irrespective of that person's seniority; (ii) any other person who performs a public function, including for a public agency or public enterprise, or provides a public service, as defined in the domestic law of the state party and as applied in the pertinent area of law of that state party; (iii) any other person defined as a 'public official' in the domestic law of a state party. However, for the purpose of some specific measures contained in Chapter II of this convention, 'public official' may mean any person who performs a public function or provides a public service as defined in the domestic law of the state party and as applied in the pertinent area of law of that state party." FATF, Recommendation 6, reads, "Financial institutions should, in relation to politically exposed persons, in addition to performing normal due diligence measures (a) have appropriate risk management systems to determine whether the customer is a politically exposed person, (b) obtain senior management approval for establishing business relationships with such customers, (c) take reasonable measures to establish the source of wealth and source of funds, (d) conduct enhanced ongoing monitoring of the business relationship."

19. UNCAC, Article 52, states, "Without prejudice to Article 14 of this convention, each state party shall take such measures as may be necessary, in accordance with its domestic law, to require financial institutions within its jurisdiction to verify the identity of customers, to take reasonable steps to determine the identity of beneficial owners of funds deposited into high-value accounts, and to conduct enhanced scrutiny of accounts sought or maintained by or on behalf of individuals who are, or have been, entrusted with

family and associates are found to have been complicit in hiding the proceeds of corruption, they may be subject to prosecution for collateral offenses such as aiding and abetting or money laundering. It is important that the proceeds of corruption held by individuals charged with collateral offenses be subject to seizure.

2.2.2 Period of Interest or Period of Check

The "period of interest" refers to the period during which a person can be held liable for having illicitly enriched himself or herself. The clear delineation of a period of interest is intended to establish a nexus between the significant increase in wealth and the person of interest's engagement in the public sector (or activities of public interest). The definition or demarcation of a period of interest may also serve a practical purpose in setting a baseline for investigators. National authorities have adopted three approaches in determining the period of interest: coincidence with the performance of functions, a limited term after leaving their functions, and an open-ended period. Lessons learned from these various approaches demonstrate that the period of check generally overlaps with part of the public official's term in office.

Although UNCAC does not specifically recommend a temporal application of illicit enrichment, one may deduce that the reference to "public official" implies that, at minimum, the period of interest coincides with the public official's performance of his functions. This approach is also adopted in the IACAC and in many national laws. Chile, for example, makes illicit enrichment applicable to a public official "who during his term" receives substantial and unjustified enrichment, thus limiting investigations to public officials who may have been enriched while in office.[20] El Salvador has a similar limitation, specifying that illicit enrichment can only be presumed when the increase in assets occurs "from the date on which the functionary took office to the day he ceased his functions."[21] Following this approach, prosecutors may use entry into functions as a baseline and assess whether increases in assets were significant in relation to the public official's lawful earnings during the performance of his or her functions or term of office. The downside of this approach is that, to avoid prosecution, a corrupt official may simply defer receiving a benefit until after leaving office.

Some countries have sought to resolve this problem by extending the period of interest for several years after the public official has terminated his or her functions or term of office. Argentina, Colombia, and Panama, for instance, have extended the period of interest to include two to five years after leaving office.[22] Other countries have left the

---

prominent public functions and their family members and close associates. Such enhanced scrutiny shall be reasonably designed to detect suspicious transactions for the purpose of reporting to competent authorities and should not be so construed as to discourage or prohibit financial institutions from doing business with any legitimate customer." For FATF, Recommendation 6, see note 7.

20. Chile, Penal Code, Article 241.

21. El Salvador, Ley Sobre el Enriquecimiento Ilícito de Funcionarios y Empleados Públicos, Título III del Enriquecimiento Ilícito.

22. Argentine Criminal Code of 1964, Article 268(2), "Any person who, when so demanded, fails to justify the origin of any appreciable enrichment for himself or a third party in order to hide it, obtained

period of interest open-ended so that anyone who has ever been a public official may be held liable for an illicit enrichment offense for the rest of his or her life. Brunei Darassalam, for example, makes illicit enrichment applicable to "any person, who, being or having been a public officer ... maintains a standard of living above that which is commensurate with his present or past emoluments." Suggestions along both of these lines were made at the time that the UNCAC was negotiated but did not receive sufficient support for inclusion in the convention.[23]

The period of interest should be distinguished from the period forming the basis of an investigation or indictment. In other words, the period identified by the illicit enrichment legislation as that during which a public official can be held liable for enriching himself may be different from the time frame for which he is actually prosecuted. The latter may be determined by the investigator and prosecutor and be equal to or fall within the period of interest.[24]

In the context of conducting investigations and cases, two challenges are worth noting: access to records and focus of investigative resources. In most countries, citizens, corporations, and financial institutions are not required to retain financial records and documentation indefinitely. Therefore, the longer the period subject to potential investigation, the higher the likelihood that any records of suspicious assets will have changed hands or been liquidated and the higher the likelihood that expenses incurred over a given period will be harder to prove. Further, if examining an extended period, prosecutors may have difficulty identifying legitimate sources of wealth, and the accused may have difficulty providing rebuttal evidence. Care should also be taken to ensure that long periods of interest do not fall outside any statutes of limitation.

Concerns regarding the period of interest may be addressed by providing specific guidance to prosecutors through administrative instructions. These instructions can,

---

subsequent to assumption of a public office or employment, and for up to two years after having ceased his duties, shall be punished." Translation from OAS (2009c). The original is presented in appendix A.
Colombian Penal Code, Article 412, states, "Any public servant who, while in government employment, or anyone who has performed public duties and who, in that time or in a period of two years thereafter, obtains for themselves or for another an unjustified increase in wealth shall, provided that the conduct does not constitute another offense, be liable to between ninety-six (96) and one hundred eighty (180) months of imprisonment, a fine of twice the amount of the enrichment without that exceeding fifty thousand (50,000) times the statutory monthly minimum wage in force, and ineligibility from the exercise of rights and public duties for between ninety-six (96) and one hundred eighty (180) months." Translation from OAS (2010c). The original is presented in appendix A.
Penal Code of Panama of 2008, Article 345, states, "Any public servant who, either personally or through a third party, unduly increases their wealth in relation to the legitimate income obtained during the occupation of their post and for up to five years after having left the post, whose lawful provenance they are unable to show, shall be punished with three to six years of imprisonment. Translation from OAS (2010g). The original is presented in appendix A.
23. UNODC (2010, 197). Ultimately, the option of extending illicit enrichment beyond employment was not retained in the final text of Article 20 of the UNCAC.
24. See *State of Maharashtra v. Pollonji Darabshaw Daruwalla*, 1988 AIR 88; 1988 SCR (1) 906; 1987 SCC Supl. 379; JT 1987 (4) 363; 1987 SCALE (2) 1127.

for instance, highlight the difficulties that are likely to be encountered in pursuing investigations once the statutory requirement has expired for citizens, corporations, and financial institutions to retain supporting documents for their financial records. This practice is consistent with the administrative guidelines used in many countries to direct prosecutors on the performance of their duties and the handling of specific cases, such as whether to begin, continue, abstain from, or stop prosecution, while fully respecting prosecutorial discretion. It is also consistent with the recommendations for the financial sector's monitoring of politically exposed persons.

2.2.3 Significant Increase in Assets

The UNCAC, IACAC, and the AUCPCC all require the prosecution to demonstrate enrichment in terms of a "significant increase in assets." According to the Travaux Preparatoires of the UNCAC, the word "significant" was retained in that particular provision, as it reflected existing practice in several states and provided further reassurance that the provisions of the article would not be used unreasonably (UNODC 2010, fn. 14). There are two considerations in defining this element: first, how to determine whether the increase in assets or wealth is "significant" and, second, which assets or other evidence will be taken into account.

The international conventions and national legislation define "significant" as a relative rather than an absolute term. For example, the increase in assets is compared with lawful sources of income using terms such as "disproportionate assets," "assets not commensurate with lawful income," or assets "above what is commensurate." Most countries do not define what is considered "disproportionate" in legislation, thus leaving this to be determined by prosecutors and the courts.

India, for instance, has set a threshold of 10 percent known sources of income through its jurisprudence.[25] A few countries provide some guidance in the form of graduated sanctions, although in these cases the thresholds are generally set in absolute terms.

Specifying a threshold for illicit enrichment in statutes may prevent prosecutions where the amounts concerned are trivial. However, it may also send a signal that a certain level of corrupt conduct will be tolerated, unless the threshold sets an extremely low bar. In those countries where the prosecutor has some discretion, public signaling can be avoided by providing policy guidance to prosecutors indicating the threshold levels at which they will be expected to prosecute. This has the advantage of providing some flexibility for prosecutors to pursue cases in exceptional circumstances if these fall below the threshold. In Pakistan, the anticorruption authority adopts an alternative approach. In order to focus time and resources on investigating major cases, as a policy, petty cases involving very small amounts of money are referred to the department concerned. The department may deal with the public official internally, may refer the case

---

25. See *Krishnanand Agnahatri v. State of M.P.* (1977), 1 SCC 816; *State of Maharashtra v. Pollonji Darabshaw Daruwalla*, 1988 AIR 88, 1988 SCR (1) 906, 1987 SCC Supl. 379, JT 1987 (4) 363, 1987 SCALE (2) 1127; *Saran v. State of M.P.*, CRA 1060/2004 (2006), INMPHC 274 (11 November 2006).

to another investigative agency, or may deal with each situation on a case-by-case basis. In some countries, there may be little need for policy guidance, as smaller thresholds may not be prosecutable under the principle of *de minimis non curat praetor* (the law does not concern itself with trifles), which bars the prosecution of minimal transgressions. In addition, smaller thresholds are more difficult for the prosecution to prove and may therefore provide fewer benefits.

Some countries have defined the type of benefit enjoyed by the public official, which is considered as part of this element of illicit enrichment. Again, where countries have included definitions, they have tended to be broad. In Argentina, the provision defines enrichment in terms of net worth, taking into account debts or other obligations that have been canceled. Paraguay also makes reference to rights granted, services provided, and the cancellation of debts not just of the accused, but also of his or her spouse and first- and second-degree bloodline relatives. In Hong Kong SAR, China, the provision also focuses on the "control" of pecuniary resources or disproportionate assets.

Countries that use the terms "standard of living" or "lifestyle" do not intend them as a substitute for assets or wealth. Rather, the "lifestyle" triggers an investigation, and the wealth of the individual remains the basis of the evidence of illicit enrichment. Some countries, such as Lesotho and Malawi, refer in their illicit enrichment laws to a "standard of living" above that which is commensurate with known sources of income rather than assets or wealth. Nepal uses the term "incompatible or unsuitable lifestyle."[26]

In that sense, the terms "lifestyle" or "standard of living" are not, strictly speaking, elements of the crime. Nonetheless, it is important to call attention to the "standard of living" or "lifestyle" because this is the visible manifestation of illicit enrichment and may lead to the filing of complaints.

The precise definition of the particular assets that are subject to illicit enrichment investigations is also an important consideration because it may determine the ease or difficulty with which the prosecution proves its case. For example, some provisions such as the illicit enrichment provision in Jamaica refer to assets disproportionate to "lawful earnings," while others refer to "official emoluments," as in Antigua and Barbuda and Hong Kong SAR, China (see appendix A). Malawi defines "official emoluments" as including "a pension, gratuity, or other terminal benefits." Therefore, because "lawful earnings" are broader than "official emoluments," it would likely be easier for the prosecution to demonstrate official emoluments through the official or departmental records than to demonstrate that the assets are disproportionate to all of his lawful earnings. In India, the illicit enrichment provision refers to "pecuniary resources or property disproportionate to his known sources of income." Although seemingly broad, the term "pecuniary resources or property" has been interpreted by the courts in India to include real property, liquid assets, and income-generating investments, while "known" has been interpreted by the courts to mean "lawfully obtained income that is revealed by a 'thorough investigation,' by the prosecution [and] cannot refer to sources of income

---

26. Nepal Prevention of Corruption Act, Article 20.

especially within the knowledge of the accused."[27] In addition, jointly held bank accounts are assessed as resources of the accused, unless the account is so structured as to prevent its use by the public official.[28]

The criticism leveled at the "significant increase in assets" is that the conventions and legislation are not explicit with regard to the criminal conduct (*actus reus*) that constitutes the basis of the offense. In Argentina, commentators have argued that Provision Article 268(2) of the Penal Code, which defines the illicit enrichment offense, fails to satisfy the principle of *nulla poena sine lege*, or no penalty without a law, enshrined in Article 18 of the constitution, which requires that legislation should clearly define the prohibited conduct or omission.[29] It has been argued, in respect of Mexico's illicit enrichment law, that the failure to define a specific conduct means that illicit enrichment penalizes the mere possession of wealth by a public servant and the suspicion of misconduct and is therefore clearly unconstitutional (Diaz-Aranda 2008, 98–100). The illicit enrichment law in Hong Kong SAR, China has been criticized on similar grounds as a draconian measure that does not constitute "a corruption crime as such but rather penalizes a public official for excess wealth *per se*" (Wilsher 2006, 31).[30]

Another interpretation is that the criminal conduct in the offense relates to the failure to justify: the offense targets an omission rather than a conduct. According to this view, a public official has a statutory duty to explain the origin of his wealth, and the failure to do so when required is an offense. Other international norms are silent on the question of what conduct should properly be regulated by criminal law. As a result, because international norms do not specify conduct that ought not to be criminalized, it cannot be said on this basis alone that illicit enrichment contravenes general principles of criminal law.

As a result, some proponents argue that the enrichment and the possession of questionable proceeds by public officials are in themselves criminal conduct. The receipt, investment, and use of the proceeds acquired by questionable means require the active participation of the public official. Property has to be purchased, maintained, and used, and bank accounts have to be opened and used for transactions. There are obvious parallels with the offense of money laundering and the possession of drugs and arms.

The most obvious lesson learned by analyzing the process of precisely describing what constitutes a "significant increase in assets" in illicit enrichment legislation is that it appears very useful to define the nature of the benefit considered as part of the increase, including, for instance, debt cancellation. The precise definition of the assets that are subject to illicit enrichment investigations, such as "official emoluments" or assets disproportionate to "lawful earnings," is also an important consideration, as the definition

---

27. The language employed by the court is drawn from §106 of the Indian Evidence Act (1872).
28. *State of Maharashtra v. Pollonji Darabshaw Daruwalla,* 1988 AIR 88; 1988 SCR (1) 906; 1987 SCC Supl. 379; JT 1987 (4) 363; 1987 SCALE (2)1127.
29. This argument is addressed in further detail in chapter 3.
30. See also the discussion on the principle of legality in chapter 3.

will determine the ease or difficulty with which the prosecution proves its case. Overall, providing details on this element goes a long way toward clarifying what conduct is considered as illicit enrichment.

2.2.4 Intent

The UNCAC explicitly requires a demonstration of the *mens rea* or intent in the offense of illicit enrichment by incorporating the element "when committed intentionally." According to the Travaux Preparatoires of the UNCAC, during negotiations of the convention, the qualification "when committed intentionally" was added to bring UNCAC, Article 20, in line with other articles in Chapter III on criminalization and to provide an additional measure of reassurance that the provisions of the article would not be used unreasonably (UNODC 2010, fn. 12). Following the principles laid out in Article 28 of the UNCAC,[31] the state of mind of the accused need not be demonstrated but instead can be inferred from the "objective factual circumstances" of the case. In illicit enrichment cases, this inference may be drawn, for instance, from significant transfers of funds from individuals or entities with which the public official has no legitimate business relationship, large cash payments made by the public official, or the continued and deliberate use of luxurious properties inexplicably acquired.

Apart from the UNCAC, none of the international or domestic laws criminalizing illicit enrichment examined in this study, including IACAC and AUCPCC, expressly identify intent as an element of the crime. This omission should not necessarily be considered as the aim of the legislature, as intent is usually considered an overarching element in the definition of criminal offenses within a criminal code and, as such, does not need to be spelled out in each and every case. In this respect, it is worth noting that both the IACAC and AUCPCC do not specify intent as an element applicable to other corruption offenses. Indeed, in some common law countries, there is a presumption that intent should be read into provisions defining the elements of crimes where they are otherwise silent.[32]

However, some commentators have argued that there may be grounds for specifically omitting intent in the context of illicit enrichment by public officials. The purposeful omission of intent as an element of the crime would transform illicit enrichment into a strict liability offense, allowing for the prosecution of an official even if he is genuinely ignorant of the unexplained income and increase in net worth. Typically, strict liability is used to prevent the accused from escaping liability by pleading ignorance, where society wishes to prevent harm and maximize the deterrent value of the offense. In the case of illicit enrichment, however, it is likely that the accused can escape liability by providing evidence of ignorance, for example, where, unknown to him, funds are accidentally deposited into his savings account and are not withdrawn.

---

31. UNCAC, Article 28, states, "Knowledge, intent, or purpose required as an element of an offense established in accordance with this convention may be inferred from objective factual circumstances."
32. *Sweet v. Parsley* (1970), AC 132.

At the national level, similar questions have been raised about the omission of intent in the statutory definition of the offense. Omission of intent in the illicit enrichment law in Hong Kong SAR, China, for example, has been interpreted by commentators as establishing strict liability for public officials. Although this approach has been put down to "poor drafting" and been criticized as a draconian measure that does not constitute "a corruption crime as such but rather penalizes a public official for excess wealth per se," the courts implementing the provision have taken a different approach (Wilsher 2006, 31). In one case in Hong Kong SAR, China, notwithstanding the absence of "intention" in the illicit enrichment provision, the court acknowledged intention as an element of the offense. It considered the fact that the accused knew that he would be unable to give a satisfactory explanation for the source of funds as *mens rea*.[33]

It is worth considering that the intent at stake in the illicit enrichment offense is related not to any misconduct, but to the increase in assets. Although most illicit enrichment provisions do not specifically mention intent, a review of existing jurisprudence revealed that such intent is a necessary factor that must be established either expressly or at least implicitly by the prosecution. Furthermore, practitioners consulted during the course of this study from both civil and common law jurisdictions agreed that convictions for illicit enrichment in their jurisdictions would require facts demonstrating this element.

2.2.5 Absence of Justification

The UNCAC, IACAC, and AUCPCC all identify the lack of a reasonable justification for the enrichment as an essential element of the illicit enrichment offense, defining it as "a significant increase in the assets of a public official that *he or she* cannot reasonably explain." The formulation of this element is considered by many to place a burden of proof on the public official. This is the most controversial of the elements, because arguments that the concept of illicit enrichment infringes on the fundamental principle of the presumption of innocence hinge on the view that the burden of proof shifts from the prosecutor to the accused (Low, Bjorklund, and Atkinson 1998). Because the legislation reviewed is generally silent on this issue, the distribution of the burden of proof in illicit enrichment cases has been determined by the courts.

In general, the practice is as follows: the prosecution constructs a case against a person who during the period of interest is a public official. The prosecution demonstrates the enrichment or ownership of assets that are significantly higher in value than the public official's lawful income. It further demonstrates that the public official had the requisite intent to be enriched. Once these elements have been established, a rebuttable presumption that this enrichment is illicit arises. A rebuttable presumption is an assumption made by a court that is taken to be true unless evidence is presented to the contrary. Therefore, once the prosecution has carried out these steps, the outcome of the case is dictated by the defense. If the accused demonstrates the existence of a reasonable explanation, he or she is acquitted; if the accused fails to do so, he or she is convicted. Figure 2.1 portrays this sequence of events.

---

33. The Privy Council in Mok Wei Tak and Another v. The Queen (1990), 2 AC 333.

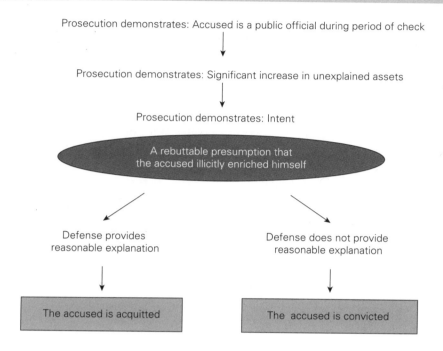

FIGURE 2.1   General Sequence of Events in an Illicit Enrichment Case

Prosecution demonstrates: Accused is a public official during period of check

Prosecution demonstrates: Significant increase in unexplained assets

Prosecution demonstrates: Intent

A rebuttable presumption that the accused illicitly enriched himself

Defense provides reasonable explanation

Defense does not provide reasonable explanation

The accused is acquitted

The accused is convicted

As to the precise nature of the prosecution's burden, courts in Argentina have repeatedly held that "the prosecution burdens the entire onus of proof."[34] This includes the presentation of evidence demonstrating that legitimate sources or official emoluments cannot account for the "disproportion" in wealth. In one case, the court said that the lack of justification does not stem from the request to the official, but results from finding that the enrichment is not supported by the declared assets of the agent. In other words, the reasonable explanation must be made only once significant and unjustified enrichment has been demonstrated. As such, the offense is committed prior to and independent of the legal requirement of justification.[35] Indian courts have also held that the burden of demonstrating assets disproportionate to known income, without a satisfactory explanation, rests with the prosecution.[36] In essence, the charge sheet must demonstrate the existence of disproportionate assets.[37]

---

34. Maria J. Alsogaray, Cámara Nacional de Casación Penal (National Chamber of Criminal Appeals), 9 June 2005; Joseph M. Pico and K.B.U., Cámara Nacional de Casación Penal (National Chamber of Criminal Appeals), 8 May 2000.

35. Maria J. Alsogaray, Cámara Nacional de Casación Penal (National Chamber of Criminal Appeals), 9 June 2005.

36. See, for example, *Bhogilal Saran v. State of M.P.,* CRA 1060/2004 (2006), INMPHC 274 (11 November 2006); *N. Ramakrishnaiah TR.LRS v. State of Andhra Pradesh* (2008), INSC 1767 (17 October 2008).

37. *Swamy v. the State,* AIR 1960 SC 7, holding that the prosecution must lay out a prima facie case of assets disproportionate to known sources of income; *Swapan Adh v. Republic of India,* CRMC no. 2008 of 1998

Hong Kong SAR, China, has made similar arguments, stating in *Attorney General v. Hui Kin-hong*, "Before the prosecution can rely on the presumption that pecuniary resources or property were in the accused's control, it has of course to prove beyond reasonable doubt the facts which give rise to it. The presumption must receive a restrictive construction, so that those facts must make it more likely than not that the pecuniary resources or property were held ... on behalf of the accused or were acquired as a gift from him."[38]

According to the general rule in many legal systems, the standard of proof in criminal matters is that an accused simply has to raise a reasonable doubt or ensure that the judge is "intimately convinced" of the weakness of the facts supporting one or more of the elements in the prosecution's case. In most cases, an accused can defend himself by presenting a plausible alternative theory of the origin of the funds with some supporting— but not highly convincing—evidence. Similarly, the accused is not required to argue in his own defense, and no adverse inference can be drawn should he choose not to.

The prosecution of illicit enrichment adopts a slightly different approach. There is an expectation that the accused will provide a reasonable explanation of a significant increase in his assets. The key consideration is the nature of the burden of proof that falls on the accused. Two alternatives are frequently argued by legal practitioners and academics alike (Jayawickrama, Pope, and Stolpe 2002, 28).

The first places an *evidentiary* burden of proof on the accused, requiring him to provide evidence that brings into question the truth of the presumed facts as presented by the prosecutor. Parallels have been drawn between the possibility for an accused to present evidence of the lawful origin of his wealth and the defense of necessity or self-defense in the context of other crimes (Godinho 2009). The burden of proof remains with the prosecution, which must demonstrate its case beyond a reasonable doubt or intimate conviction and refute the evidence provided by the accused. However, when there is an evidentiary burden on the accused, adverse inferences may be drawn from the failure of the accused to provide evidence in his or her own defense. A clear statutory example in Pakistan provides,

> In any trial of an offense punishable under this order, the fact that the accused person or any other person on his behalf, is in possession, for which the accused person cannot satisfactorily account, of property or pecuniary resources disproportionate to his known sources of income, or that such person has, at or about the time of the commission of the

---

(2000), INORHC 179 (23 March 2000), assuming that the prosecution had met its burden, the charge sheet could not be challenged with evidence until the case was brought to trial; *State by Central Bureau of Investigation v. Shri S. Bangarappa* (2000), INSC 578 (20 November 2000), finding that the presiding judge need not evaluate the quality of the prosecution's evidence, provided that on its face the evidence presented constituted a prima facie case; *State of Madhya Pradesh v. Mohanlal Soni* (2000), INSC 362 (19 July 2000), in which the prosecution failed to review adequately and make available relevant documentation that would have discredited the prosecution's alleged prima facie case, quashing the proceeding; *Parkash Singh Badal and Anr v. State of Punjab and Ors* (2006), INSC 906 (6 December 2006), allowing for the charge sheet to allege a violation of §13.1, without specifying which offense is alleged.
38. *Attorney General v. Hui Kin Hong*, Court of Appeal no. 52 of 1995.

offense with which he is charged, obtained an accretion to his pecuniary resources or property for which he cannot satisfactorily account, *the court shall presume, unless the contrary is proved, that the accused person is guilty of the offense of corruption and/or corrupt practices and his conviction therefore shall not be invalid by reason only that it is based solely on such a presumption.*[39]

The second alternative considered in arguments regarding illicit enrichment places a *legal* burden of proof on the accused. The general rule in criminal cases is that the prosecution bears the legal burden of proving the accused person's guilt. However, where the legal burden of proof is on the accused, the burden of proving an element must be discharged by the accused. The accused has to prove his defense on a balance of probabilities. Should the defense merely raise a reasonable doubt as to the accused person's guilt, but fail to convince the court on a balance of probabilities that the presumed fact is untrue, the accused is found guilty. According to this view, where a legal burden of proof is placed on the accused, the accused person's failure to provide rebutting evidence automatically results in a conviction.

Courts have generally moved toward placing an evidentiary burden of proof on the accused once the prosecution has established its case. In India, for instance, courts have held that the justification should present a "satisfactory account" built on "cogent evidence."[40] A satisfactory account should be not only "plausible" but also "convincing."[41] "Cogent evidence" has been held to mean something more than testimony of a public official, even when this testimony is corroborated.[42] There is a marked preference for documentary evidence of the legitimate source of wealth. A similar approach is seen in Egypt, where the official is required to present documentation of legitimate sources of income. In this respect, it is worth noting that public servants are usually paid by bank transfer or check, are administratively attached to a ministry that manages their career, and can provide access to the required documentation necessary to verify their official income. Their tax documentation is also a relevant element and should be consistent with their wealth; therefore, such documentation may help them to prove their legitimate sources of income.

In practice, when an accused offers a reasonable explanation in court, he also provides his defense, which may, depending on the jurisdiction and the court, constitute a reasonable explanation. Defenses may include, among other things, a claim that the increased assets were the result of an inheritance, a gift from relatives and close associates, remittances received from abroad from close relatives, or prize money.

---

39. Emphasis added. National Accountability Ordinance, Section 14(c).
40. See, for example, *Swamy v. the State*, AIR 1960 SC 7; *Saran v. State of M.P.*, CRA 1060/2004 (2006), INMPHC 274 (11 November 2006); and *N. Ramakrishnaiah TR.LRS v. State of Andhra Pradesh* (2008), INSC 1767 (17 October 2008).
41. *N. Ramakrishnaiah TR.LRS v. State of Andhra Pradesh* (2008), INSC 1767 (17 October 2008).
42. Compare *Sajjan Singh v. the State of Punjab*, 1964 AIR 464, 1964 SCR (4) 630, and *K. Dhanalakshmi v. State*, Crl.A.1158 of 2000 (2007), INTNHC 1990 (19 June 2006), with *Chennai v. K. Inbasagaran*, Appeal (crl.) 480 of 2002. However, in *Saran v. State of M.P.*, CRA 1060/2004 (2006), INMPHC 274 (11 November 2006), the court held that testimony from multiple persons was sufficient to overcome the prosecution's alleged percentage of income devoted to household expenditures, which was not supported by evidence.

Some defenses are specific to certain countries and take advantage of the weaknesses in a country's financial and legal infrastructure. For example, in Pakistan taxes on agricultural proceeds are not always imposed or enforced, so agricultural proceeds tend to be proffered as a defense because this is harder to challenge. Similarly, the contention that money consisted of prize bond winnings is frequently accepted in Pakistan, even though there is a strong possibility that the accused purchased the prize bonds from another person. At the end of the day, as in any penal trial, the judges will assess the credibility of an accused person's arguments.

2.3 Observations

While there are common elements to the illicit enrichment provisions in different jurisdictions, states considering enacting such legislation will be poorly served by adopting "model" legislation or drawing uncritically on the definitions applied in other jurisdictions. Overall, lessons learned from states implementing illicit enrichment provisions demonstrate that an appropriate formulation of the elements will ultimately depend on the legal and procedural systems available in each country and should be determined through the legislative and judicial process.

This process will need to consider illicit enrichment in the broader context of the criminalization of corruption, the oversight regime for public officials, the specific objectives to be achieved with the illicit enrichment offense, and the nature of guidance that can be remitted to supporting regulations and administrative instructions. Therefore, in deciding the components of the illicit enrichment offense in each jurisdiction, the language of the relevant statutory provision is crucial. As a general rule, it is helpful for the legislation to be as specific as possible in defining the elements of the case so as to clarify the objectives of the legislators and the roles of the court, prosecution, and defense when dealing with an illicit enrichment offense. Accordingly, jurisdictions that consider the reasonable explanation a defense may find it helpful to specify this in the provision.

3. Human Rights and Constitutional Aspects

Human rights and constitutional arguments often arise in discussions surrounding the criminalization of illicit enrichment. At the outset, one should note that human rights are universal and apply to all human beings, while constitutional rights are specific to particular jurisdictions. Under international human rights law,[43] states have the duty to respect, protect, and fulfill their human rights obligations. This also applies to all substantive aspects of an offense, including illicit enrichment. Accordingly, it has been recognized that "effective anticorruption measures and the protection of human rights are mutually reinforcing and that the promotion and protection of human rights is essential to the fulfillment of all aspects of an anticorruption strategy."[44]

A human rights–based approach to illicit enrichment requires that all measures addressing this issue conform with the state's international human rights obligations. Of particular relevance is Article 2 of the 1966 International Covenant on Civil and Political Rights (ICCPR)[45] with respect to legislative, administrative, and judicial measures, which implies the development of institutions related to investigations, prosecutions, and adjudication of corruption-related offenses such as illicit enrichment. Human rights aspects of the legal framework for illicit enrichment should also take a holistic approach, encompassing the criminal justice system of each jurisdiction.

This need is due in large part to constitutional and human rights concerns that the offense of illicit enrichment has not been adopted as a universal standard. Arguments

---

43. See http://www.ohchr.org/EN/ProfessionalInterest/Pages/InternationalLaw.aspx.
44. Human Rights Council, Resolution 7/11 of 27 March 2008, on the role of good governance in promoting and protecting human rights.
45. ICCPR, Article 2, states, "1. Each state party to the present covenant undertakes to respect and to ensure to all individuals within its territory and subject to its jurisdiction the rights recognized in the present covenant, without distinction of any kind, such as race, colour, sex, language, religion, political or other opinion, national or social origin, property, birth, or other status. 2. Where not already provided for by existing legislative or other measures, each state party to the present covenant undertakes to take the necessary steps, in accordance with its constitutional processes and with the provisions of the present covenant, to adopt such laws or other measures as may be necessary to give effect to the rights recognized in the present covenant. 3. Each state party to the present covenant undertakes (a) to ensure that any person whose rights or freedoms as herein recognized are violated shall have an effective remedy, notwithstanding that the violation has been committed by persons acting in an official capacity; (b) to ensure that any person claiming such a remedy shall have his right thereto determined by competent judicial, administrative, or legislative authorities, or by any other competent authority provided for by the legal system of the state, and to develop the possibilities of judicial remedy; (c) to ensure that the competent authorities shall enforce such remedies when granted."

in this context have turned on whether the prosecution of illicit enrichment requires an impermissible shift or a partial reversal of the burden of proof and whether it entails presumptions similar to those recognized in numerous other offenses.

In view of such concerns, some state parties to the United Nations Convention against Corruption (UNCAC), the Inter-American Convention against Corruption (IACAC), and the African Union Convention on Preventing and Combating Corruption (AUCPCC) choose not to criminalize the offense in their jurisdictions under the safeguard clauses of these instruments, which allow states subject to the constitutions, laws, and the fundamental principles of their systems to determine whether or not to implement parts of international conventions. In some countries, such as Portugal, where the enactment of illicit enrichment has been considered, but not yet implemented, debates have focused on constitutional and human rights issues. Critics have gone so far as to argue that the offense of illicit enrichment is so flawed that it is "a remedy that is worse than the ailment" and that the criminalization of illicit enrichment should be discouraged in an environment with weak governance.[46]

Rule of law is integral to and indispensable for good governance, citizens' security, development, and human rights. A weaker of rule of law suggests a lower probability of catching a corrupt public agent. Unfortunately, jurisdictions with a pressing need to stamp out corruption often also have a pressing need to strengthen their rule of law. Some commentators critical of the criminalization of illicit enrichment also note that prosecutorial discretion, where it is open to abuse, may further add to the concerns. In this respect, a broader understanding of the criminal justice system, its independence from political pressure, and its institutional and technical capacity is important when considering whether and how to enact illicit enrichment statutes.

Apart from the concerns surrounding the rule of law, this study found that many developing countries where corruption is perceived as pervasive have been willing to implement the illicit enrichment offense in order to tackle the problem with the entire range of tools available. This is also supported by the rule of law ranking of these jurisdictions in the Worldwide Governance Indicators of 2009 prepared by the World Bank Institute. Appendix B of this study provides a list of jurisdictions with illicit enrichment provisions and their rankings on the rule of law, control of corruption, and GDP per capita. The situation in Hong Kong SAR, China, further illustrates this point: the illicit enrichment provision was introduced when corruption was widespread in the public sector, most notably the police force. Now that the perception of corruption has declined, it is used less frequently. In the final analysis, as long as measures are taken

---

46. According to Snider and Kidane (2007, 728), it is "highly doubtful that compromising the fundamental principle of the presumption of innocence in the interest of combating unexplained material gains by government officials is a desirable course. This is particularly true in Africa where, as the African Union Corruption Convention suggests, the crime of corruption is directly linked with the rule of law and good governance. In fact, it directly conflicts with the principles enshrined under recognized universal human rights instruments as well as the African Charter on Human and Peoples' Rights. The implementation of this provision as written in the domestic sphere should not be encouraged, because it might mean prescribing a remedy that is worse than the ailment."

within the context of Article 2 of the ICCPR to ensure that the rule of law is observed in these circumstances, illicit enrichment provisions can still be applied properly.

In many countries that have implemented illicit enrichment, convictions have been challenged on constitutional and human rights grounds. In some countries, these challenges have been successful and illicit enrichment has been held as unconstitutional. In 1994, Italy's Constitutional Court overturned the illicit enrichment provisions of Law no. 356 of 1992 on grounds that a presumption based on the status of the accused violated the presumption of innocence.[47] In 2004 in the Arab Republic of Egypt, the Cassation Court addressed the question of whether the illicit wealth offense is compatible with legal principles and held that the second paragraph of Article 2 of the Illicit Enrichment Law, which defines as an offense whenever such increase is not consistent with the public official's resources and the public official fails to prove the legitimate source for it, violated the constitution regarding the genesis and presumption of innocence.[48]

Until 2010, the Romania National Integrity Agency (ANI) could directly request a court to confiscate unexplained assets if, following its verification procedures, it found an obvious difference (defined as more than €10,000) that could not be justified between the wealth acquired while in office and income realized during the same period of time.[49] However, in April 2010, the Constitutional Court of Romania held that several elements of that illicit enrichment law violated the constitution. The court found that the power of ANI to ask courts to confirm and confiscate significant unjustified differences between the income and acquired assets of public officials breached the constitutional prohibition on the confiscation of legally acquired property as well as the presumption of innocence.[50]

Romania has since addressed these constitutional issues and enacted a similar provision as a confiscation measure that is no longer a criminal offense.[51] ANI still evaluates if there is a significant difference of more than €10,000 between the wealth and income of a public official accumulated while in office. If the agency finds such a difference, it sends a report to different offices depending on the case: to the tax authorities, the

---

47. Case no. 48/1994.
48. The law has been amended since, and illicit enrichment, as an offense, is still used, for instance, to prosecute top-level public officials.
49. Between May 2009 and May 2010, ANI sent six files to court (for confiscation of unjustified wealth). As of May 2010, two findings of unjustified wealth had been confirmed by the courts in first instance decisions, and the confiscation of significant assets had been ordered, although both decisions have been appealed. In the first case, the court ordered the confiscation of €458,805, US$1,580, and lei 29,345. In the second case, the court ordered the confiscation of €9,750 and lei 913,591 (supporting document accompanying European Commission 2010).
50. The objection of constitutionality was raised in one of the agency's first major confiscation trials, a €3.5 million case concerning a former member of Parliament (for more on the decision of the Constitutional Court, see supporting document accompanying European Commission 2010).
51. See Law no. 176 of September 2010, which was adopted in response to the decision of the Romanian Constitutional Court.

prosecutor's office, or the Commission for the Examination of Wealth.[52] The Commission for the Examination of Wealth starts the control activities as soon as it receives the evaluation report from ANI. At the end of the control procedure, the commission can decide with a majority of votes whether to send the case to an appeals court if it concludes that the assets, in whole or in part, have an unjustified or illicit character. If the appeals court finds that the acquisition of some assets cannot be justified, it decides whether to confiscate these assets or demand a payment equal to their value.

3.1 The Main Principles at Stake

Specific arguments that illicit enrichment prosecutions violate human rights principles have included violations of the presumption of innocence, the right against self-incrimination, and the principle of legality.

3.1.1 Presumption of Innocence

The presumption of innocence is a fundamental right in human rights law, protected by all the major international and regional instruments of human rights and fundamental freedoms. Article 11(1) of the Universal Declaration of Human Rights safeguards the presumption of innocence for everyone "charged with a penal offense … until proved guilty according to law in a public trial at which he has had all the guarantees necessary for his defense." Similar principles are laid out in Article 7(1)(b) of the African Charter on Human and Peoples' Rights, Article 8(2) of the American Convention on Human Rights, and Article 6(2) of the European Convention on Human Rights.

The presumption of innocence requires the state to prove the guilt of an accused and relieves the accused of any burden to prove his or her innocence. The United Nations Human Rights Committee states, "The burden of proof of the charge is on the prosecution and the accused has the benefit of doubt. No guilt can be presumed until the charge has been proved beyond reasonable doubt [or intimate conviction]" (United Nations Office of the High Commissioner for Human Rights 1984, 124, para. 7).

In Argentina, illicit enrichment was challenged in the *Alsogaray* case on grounds that it violates the presumption of innocence.[53] In this case, the court held that the crime of illicit enrichment does not require the public official to prove his or her innocence. Instead, the public prosecutor brings evidence of the unjustified increase with the highest specificity and accuracy possible. In this case, the justification mentioned in the illicit enrichment provision does not violate the privilege against self-incrimination, as

---

52. Pursuant to Amended Law no. 115 of 1996, the Commissions for the Examination of Wealth were established under the framework of appellate courts. Each commission includes two appellate court judges and one prosecutor. The Superior Council of Magistracy informed ANI in October 2010 that the procedure for appointing the members of these commissions had started.
53. Maria J. Alsogaray, Cámara Nacional de Casación Penal (National Chamber of Criminal Appeals), June 9, 2005.

it can only be understood as a notice to the accused of the need to demonstrate the legality of his or her enrichment.[54] However, the Supreme Court in Argentina has not yet pronounced on the constitutionality of the concept of illicit enrichment.

The principle of the presumption of innocence does not exclude legislatures from creating criminal offenses containing a presumption by law as long as the principles of rationality (reasonableness) and proportionality are duly respected.

These principles have been applied in order to align the presumption of innocence with an important precedent set by the European Court of Human Rights in *Salabiaku v. France*.[55] Salabiaku was a Zairian national convicted of violating French customs law by receiving a package containing 10 kilograms of cannabis. In its decision, the court outlined its approach to the permissibility of burden-shifting provisions, an approach that can be referred to as the *Salabiaku* test. The *Salabiaku* test is based on the recognition that "presumptions of fact or of law operate in every legal system," but that states must confine presumptions "within reasonable limits which take into account the importance of what is at stake and maintain the rights of the defense."[56] Therefore, the court balanced the state's interest in the prosecution with the rights of the accused by keeping presumptions within reasonable limits.

In applying the *Salabiaku* test to illicit enrichment, the question becomes whether the public interest in convicting corrupt officials outweighs the infringement on the rights of the accused. In 1976 in the United Kingdom, the Royal Commission of Conduct in Public Life argued, "Such a burden can only be justified for compelling reasons, but we think that in the sphere of corruption the reasons are indeed compelling ... the burden of proof on the defense is in the public interest and causes no injustice" (Royal Commission of Conduct in Public Life 1976, cmnd. 6525, cited in de Speville 1997). The Court of Appeals in Hong Kong SAR, China, came to a similar conclusion in *Attorney General v. Hui Kin Hong*. While it accepted that requiring the accused to discharge the burden of proof deviates from the presumption of innocence, it held the following: "There are exceptional situations in which it is possible compatibly with human rights to justify a degree of deviation from the normal principle that the prosecution must prove the accused's guilt beyond reasonable doubt."[57]

---

54. Ibid. The Spanish original reads, in part, "El debido requerimiento que menciona la norma debe consistir en un acto de autoridad pública por el cual se le haga saber al funcionario la constatación del enriquecimiento apreciable e injustificado observado, con la mayor especificidad y precisión posibles respeto a todas sus circunstancias. Tal requerimiento tiene por objeto que el requerido pueda brindar las razones o argumentos de que la procedencia obedece a un origen legítimo ... El delito de enriquecimiento ilícito no pone en cabeza del requerido el deber de demostrar su inocencia, sino que al Ministerio Público Fiscal al que le corresponde la prueba del aumento patrimonial injustificado. El requerimiento de justificación del art. 268 (2) CP no viola la prohibición de autoincriminación en tanto aquél sólo puede ser entendido como una notificación para que el acusado pueda hacer uso de la oportunidad formal de probar la licitud de su enriquecimiento."
55. *Salabiaku v. France* (1988), Application no. 10519/83, Section 28.
56. Ibid.
57. *Attorney General v. Hui Kin Hong*, Court of Appeal no. 52 of 1995.

The effectiveness and correctness of illicit enrichment prosecutions and their compliance with due process should also be considered in the context of the criminal justice system implementing it. This includes considerations consistent with Article 2 of the ICCPR and with Article 14 concerning the right to a fair trial. It is only when these measures are fully implemented that an accused can receive a fair trial for illicit enrichment or any other offense.

3.1.2 Protection against Self-Incrimination

Protection against self-incrimination is recognized in Article 8(2)(g) of the American Convention on Human Rights, which establishes the right of the accused in a criminal case "not to be compelled to be a witness against himself or to plead guilty."[58] This right extends to the further right of the accused to remain silent.[59] Although this right is not specifically mentioned in the European Convention on Human Rights or the African Charter on Human and Peoples' Rights, the European Court of Human Rights has unequivocally held the following: "There can be no doubt that the right to remain silent under police questioning and the privilege against self-incrimination are generally recognized international standards which lie at the heart of the notion of a fair procedure." According to these principles, "A suspect must at no time, and in no circumstances, be compelled to incriminate himself or herself or to confess guilt; a suspect has the right to remain silent at all times" (University of Minnesota Human Rights Library n.d.).

The explanation provided by the defense in an illicit enrichment case does expose the accused to the risk of self-incrimination. Evidence of income from inheritances, businesses, gambling, or gifts may be exculpatory for the purposes of illicit enrichment, but it may still expose the public official to criminal, administrative, or fiscal sanctions for other offenses: for instance, where income and assets were not recorded in disclosures, the official engaged in activities or employment that are incompatible with his public functions, or income was not declared to the tax authorities. In these circumstances, accused persons may be reluctant to establish an appropriate defense or may incriminate themselves by doing so.

While a fundamental right, there is established precedent that the right against self-incrimination is not absolute. In *O'Hallaran and Francis v. the United Kingdom*,[60] the accused persons were held liable for refusing to provide records indicating who had been driving a taxi at the time of a criminal violation. The European Court of Human

---

58. See also European Court on Human Rights, *John Murray v. the United Kingdom,* Judgment of 8 February 1996, Reports 1996-I, p. 49, para. 45. The right not to be compelled to incriminate oneself and to confess guilt is also contained in Article 55(1)(a) of the Law of the International Criminal Court and in Articles 20(4)(g) and 21(4)(g) of the respective laws of the International Criminal Tribunals for Rwanda and the former Yugoslavia.

59. Article 55(2)(b) of the Law of the International Criminal Court provides that a suspect shall be informed prior to questioning that he has a right to "remain silent, without such silence being a consideration in the determination of guilt or conscience."

60. *O'Hallaran and Francis v. the United Kingdom,* Application nos. 15809/02 and 25624/02 (2007).

Rights held, "All who own or drive motor cars know that by doing so they subject themselves to a regulatory regime. This regime is imposed not because owning or driving cars is a privilege or indulgence granted by the state but because the possession and use of cars (like, for example, shotguns ...) are recognized to have the potential to cause grave injury."[61] Other examples of compulsory self-incrimination include the requirement to submit to a breathalyzer[62] and the mandatory installation of tachographs in trucks.[63]

This reasoning can be extended to public servants, who are subject to a specific regulatory regime. In assuming a position of trust, public officials subject themselves to the legal requirements and the administrative and criminal sanctions that arise from the abuse of that trust. Moreover, where countries have an established income and asset disclosure regime, they also have established the principle that public officials may provide personal information that may be self-incriminating. In this context, providing evidence regarding the sources of income and assets to the court does not appear as a significant additional burden.

Furthermore, courts have also accepted that they may draw adverse inferences where the accused has chosen to remain silent. In *Murray v. United Kingdom*, the European Court of Human Rights accepted that the court could draw adverse inferences from the accused's silence when the factual circumstances allowed doing so.[64]

3.1.3 The Principle of Legality

The principle of legality requires that an act be illegal according to the criminal law of a particular jurisdiction before it can be punished. It is included in Article 15(1) of the ICCPR, which embodies the principle *nullum crimen sine lege* (a crime must be provided for by law).[65] Some opponents of illicit enrichment argue that it violates the principle of legality, as it does not clearly define a prohibited conduct that constitutes the basis of the offense.

In a case in Argentina, the appellant argued that the illicit enrichment provision is susceptible to different interpretations and, as such, affects the principle of legality. The Supreme Court of Justice dismissed these arguments, holding that the crime of illicit enrichment is a crime of commission, as it consists of a significant and unjustified enrichment after taking public office.[66] It also held that the continuous involvement of

---

61. Ibid., 57.
62. Ibid., 31.
63. *J. B. v. Switzerland*, Application no. 31827/96 (2001).
64. *John Murray v. U.K.*, Application no. 18731/91, Judgment, 8 February 2006, paras. 47 and 51.
65. See also ICCPR, Article 9(1), which states, "No one shall be deprived of his liberty except on such grounds and in accordance with such procedure as are established by law."
66. Maria J. Alsogaray, Cámara Nacional de Casación Penal (National Chamber of Criminal Appeals), 9 June 2005. This view was upheld on appeal by the Courte Suprema de Justicia de la Nación (Supreme Court of Justice), 22 December 2008.

the accused in the case had not prevented her from knowing the act she was alleged to have committed.[67]

3.2 Legal Presumptions Contained in Offenses Other Than Illicit Enrichment

Several related presumptions exist in offenses that are applied in various jurisdictions for the purpose of prosecuting and recovering the proceeds of crime. Although similar to illicit enrichment, these offenses are not illicit enrichment and extend to other serious offenses beyond corruption. These related presumptions have been applied mainly in the recovery of the proceeds of organized crime as well as in civil proceedings. They are sometimes targeted toward depriving offenders of their ill-gotten gains, without contributing to a finding of an accused's guilt. They often do not require a link between the assets and a crime for which the individual was actually convicted. Presumptions have also been used in a wider context with regard to those who occupy positions of trust. In the United States, for instance, there is a presumption of fraud or undue influence where a guardian or the holder of a power of attorney uses the other person's assets to his or her own benefit.

The United Nations Convention on Transnational Organized Crime proposes as a means of strengthening the confiscation regime that states "may consider the possibility of requiring that an offender demonstrate the lawful origin of alleged proceeds of crime or other property liable to confiscation, to the extent that such a requirement is consistent with the principles of their domestic law and with the nature of the judicial and other proceedings."[68] This is consistent with the approach of some jurisdictions, which some view as providing for a discretionary power to reverse the burden of proof, as the offenders have to demonstrate the legal source of the property.

In Italy, Legislative Decree 306 of 8 June 1992, aimed at tackling drug trafficking and organized crime, provides that any money, goods, or profit whose source or origin cannot be justified and which belongs to someone found guilty of Mafia-related crimes can be seized when it can be shown to be the person's property, either directly or through a third person, be this an individual or a corporate body, which he has free use of and where the property is disproportionate in value to his own income. It is widely considered to place the burden of proof on the accused if the prosecution establishes that an accused person's assets are not commensurate with his legitimate sources of income and to allow for the forfeiture of all of the accused person's property.[69]

---

67. Maria J. Alsogaray, Courte Suprema de Justicia de la Nación (Supreme Court of Justice), 22 December 2008.

68. Article 12(7), Confiscation and Seizure.

69. Sections 1 and 2 of Law Decree no. 306 of 8 June 1992, supplemented by Section 2 of Law Decree no. 399 of 20 June 1994, enacted as Law no. 501 of 8 August 1994.

In France, the version of Article 321(6) of the Penal Code adopted in 2006 covers organized crime and other offenses. It can be used in corruption cases, as the predicate offenses of generating illicit gains cover a wide range of offenses. These include active and passive corruption, conflict of interest, and misuse of company assets, which are the main offenses used in France to prosecute acts of corruption. According to the article, "The failure to justify resources corresponding to one's lifestyle or to justify the origin of assets owned while in habitual relationship with one or more persons engaged in the commission of offenses punishable by at least five years of imprisonment and providing them a direct or indirect benefit, or while in habitual relationship with victims of these offenses, is punishable by three years of imprisonment and €75,000 fine." This article does not intend to penalize the corrupt official himself, but rather his associates, family members, or, more generally, those persons in habitual relationship with him. However, similarities exist with the illicit enrichment offense. The onus of proof is on a particular person only because of his or her classification as an associate, family member, or close relation. It is similar to the burden of proof required of a public official suspected of illicit enrichment due to his status.

The Council of Europe issued Framework Decision no. 2005/212/HA, Confiscation of Crime-Related Proceeds, Instrumentalities, and Properties, which aims "to ensure that all member states have effective rules governing the confiscation of proceeds from crime, *inter alia*, in relation to the onus of proof regarding the source of assets held by a person convicted of an offense related to organized crime." Member states are encouraged to enable confiscation "where it is established that the value of the property is disproportionate to the lawful income of the convicted person and a national court based on specific facts is fully convinced that the property in question has been derived from the criminal activity of that convicted person."[70]

In Germany, Criminal Code, Section 73d, is enabling legislation that shifts the burden of proof to the accused if the prosecution establishes a significant increase in the assets of a public official that have not been accounted for. The legislation requires forfeiture of assets "where there are grounds to believe that the objects were used for or obtained through unlawful acts." The Federal Supreme Court has argued that this does not reduce the burden of proof but absolves the prosecution from establishing "the specific details" of the offense.

Similarly, Article 36 of the Dutch Criminal Code allows for the confiscation of the proceeds of the crime for which the offender has been convicted as well as the confiscation of assets "which are probably derived from other criminal activities." The Supreme Court has argued that this is consistent with the presumption of innocence because "once a presumption of criminal origin of proceeds has been established by the prosecution, the defense can always reverse the presumption. Once the criminal origin of the proceeds has been made probable, the burden to rebut—not simply to deny—this presumption lies with the defense" (Stessens 2004, 71–73).

---

70. Ibid.

In Switzerland, if it is established that an individual supports or is part of a criminal organization, the court is obligated to order the confiscation of all the assets owned by that individual. Criminal Code, Article 59(3), creates a presumption that a criminal organization controls the assets of all of its members. It is then up to the individual to rebut the presumption by demonstrating the legal origin of the assets. The Supreme Court upheld the position that this respects the presumption of innocence because the accused can rebut it by demonstrating that he is not under the organization's control or the assets have legal origin (Jorge 2007, 17–21).

In Thailand, the concept of "unusual wealth" under Section 75 of the National Counter Corruption Commission Act allows the institution of a case against an individual holding a political position or any state official who has become unusually wealthy. Where a request is made that the property be ordered to devolve upon the state, the accused must prove to the court that the property does not result from the unusual wealth. The Thai Supreme Court has held that unusual wealth is an independent civil proceeding.

In Australia, the idea of penalizing unexplained wealth was first introduced by Western Australia and the Northern Territory in their Proceeds of Crime Legislation, but was absent from the federal legislation known as POCA (Proceeds of Crime Act). The POCA was enacted in 2002, and its implementation has been reviewed periodically. A 2006 review concluded, "To introduce these provisions would represent a significant step beyond the national and international consensus in this area" (Sherman 2006, 36–37). In 2009 a press release from the Australian Federal Police Association revealed support for unexplained wealth legislation citing the 1997 resolution of the International Criminal Police Organization (INTERPOL) General Assembly, which "recognized that unexplained wealth is a legitimate subject of enquiry for law enforcement institutions in their efforts to detect criminal activity and that subject to the fundamental principles of each country's domestic law, legislators should reverse the burden of proof (use the concept of reverse onus) in respect of unexplained wealth." An amendment to the POCA in 2010 finally introduced unexplained wealth as an offense at the federal level.

In addition to conviction-based forfeiture, innovative systems are being developed to facilitate asset forfeiture. Recently, Switzerland approved legislation that provides for the use of administrative forfeiture to recover the proceeds of illicit enrichment held by foreign politically exposed persons in their jurisdiction (see box 3.1).

3.3 Protection of the Rights of the Accused in Illicit Enrichment Proceedings

In certain cases, although the elements of illicit enrichment are met, conviction may be set aside on account of a procedural irregularity in order to protect the rights of the accused. One of the major arguments against criminalizing illicit enrichment is that it is an offense that can be easily abused, with accusers making allegations for political

BOX 3.1 Administrative Forfeiture in Switzerland

On October 1, 2010, the Swiss Parliament passed the Return of Illicit Assets Act, which seeks to facilitate the recovery of the proceeds of corruption in situations where the state of origin of the assets is unable to conduct a criminal procedure that meets the requirements of Swiss law on international mutual assistance. This provides for the freezing, forfeiture, and restitution of assets held by foreign politically exposed persons and their associates in Switzerland on the basis of decisions by the Federal Administrative Court. Following Article 6, the court may presume the unlawful origin of these assets where "the wealth of the person who holds powers of disposal over the assets has been subject to an extraordinary increase that is connected with the exercise of a public office by the politically exposed person and the level of corruption in the country of origin or surrounding the politically exposed person in question during their term of office is or was acknowledged as high." The court may reject the presumption "if it can be demonstrated that in all probability the assets were acquired by lawful means." Decisions of the Federal Administrative Court are subject to appeal to the Federal Supreme Court.

Justification for this law, which many consider to entail a partial reversal of the burden of proof, is found in the presumption of ownership on the grounds of possession, which is codified in Article 930 of the Swiss Civil Code. The Supreme Court has claimed that this presumption of ownership cannot be claimed if possession is "ambiguous," where the circumstances of acquisition or the exercise of authority over the property are unclear, or if there are doubts about the legal validity of the identity documents used to gain possession. In such cases, the possessor must prove that he has acquired the asset in a lawful manner.

Source: Federal Act on the Restitution of Assets of Politically Exposed Persons Obtained by Unlawful Means: Restitution of Illicit Assets Act (RIAA) of 1 October 2010. Further commentary on the law is presented in Federal Council 10.039 Dispatch Concerning the Federal Act on the Restitution of Assets of Politically Exposed Persons Obtained by Unlawful Means (Restitution of Illicit Assets Act, RIAA) of 28 April 2010.

gain. Therefore, courts have established certain exceptions as safeguards for the trial process.

In this respect, the courts will accept a plea of *mala fides*, according to which a challenge of bad faith is lodged before the courts. In the case of *Badal v. State of Punjab*,[71] the Indian Appellate Court stressed that mere allegation and suspicions are not sufficient, but should be supported by cogent evidence. It added that simply because the accuser is a political opponent does not necessarily mean that the complaint has to be thrown out or that no notice should be taken of it.

Prejudice to such a degree that it constitutes a miscarriage of justice is another basis upon which courts have vitiated illicit enrichment proceedings. In one case, the court

---

71. *Parkash Singh Badal and Anr v. State of Punjab and Ors*, INSC 906 (6 December 2006).

held that there had been a miscarriage of justice because the prosecution had withheld documents, failed to conduct a thorough investigation, and failed to file the proper order authorizing the investigation. Furthermore, these inadequacies were not adequately explained at trial.[72]

In certain jurisdictions, as in India, prior sanction is required to begin investigations. The case can be prosecuted only if the accused has been previously sanctioned by his administrative authority. This is meant as a filter to ensure that only those cases warranting investigations are pursued. However, as reported by India for the purpose of this study, this filter sometimes prevents prosecution against high-level officials, who are likely to benefit from protection and leniency from their own administration, especially in public sectors where corruption is widespread.

3.4 Observations

It would be counterproductive to put in place a criminal offense intended to reinforce the rule of law that undermines the very principles upon which that law is built. While some commentators have argued that illicit enrichment raises concerns regarding fundamental principles of law and human rights, notably regarding the burden of proof, the presumption of innocence, and the privilege against self-incrimination, experience and jurisprudence have shown that not all rights are absolute. These fundamental principles are often qualified in the application of the law to serve the interests of both the public and justice. As a result, the criminalization of illicit enrichment is a clear example of the tension between the public interest in eradicating corruption and the rights of the individual—one that each jurisdiction will have to address it in its own way.

The claim that the use of a rebuttable presumption of illicit enrichment shifts the burden of proof to the accused constitutes a narrow reading of the elements of the offense. Furthermore, the European Court of Human Rights has accepted, in principle (though not in jurisprudence related to illicit enrichment per se), that it may be appropriate to use rebuttable presumptions that shift some of the evidentiary burden of proof to the accused where the legislature has decided that this would be in the public interest, as determined by the court, taking into account the facts of the case and being within reasonable limits that respect the rights of the defense. Similarly, the same court has accepted that those accused may be required to provide evidence overriding their right against self-incrimination where this is in the public interest.

In sum, the lessons learned from the jurisprudence described here show that, to protect human rights when addressing any shift in the burden of proof in an illicit enrichment offense, it is important to consider the rationality of the offense and the proportionality of the sanction. Domestic courts and the European Court of Human Rights both have recognized that any breach in human rights principles, such as the presumption of

---

72. *State Inspector of Police Viskhapatnam v. Surya Sankaram Karri* (2006), RD-SC 520 (24 August 2006).

innocence and protection against self-incrimination, can be acceptable if rationality and proportionality criteria are met.

While rigorous adherence to the law and legal procedures are essential for the defense of the constitution, the rule of law, and human rights, these objectives cannot be ensured through legislation alone. In fact, effective, transparent, and independent institutions for the administration of justice are equally important. States have also recognized that transparent, accountable, and participatory government, which is responsive to the needs and aspirations of the people, is the foundation upon which good governance rests. They have further noted that such a foundation is an indispensable condition for the full realization of human rights, including the right to development.[73]

Lessons learned by states that have prosecuted illicit enrichment in this respect are that, with proper legal and institutional safeguards in place, illicit enrichment provisions can be an effective tool that is used fairly. The challenge for national authorities is to develop the institutional capacity to assert independence and to be vigilant against potential abuse. In many developing countries, this may require investments in building the capacity of prosecutors, the judiciary, and law enforcement while ensuring their independence and impartiality.

---

73. European Court of Human Rights Resolution 7/11 of 27 March 2008.

4. Operational Aspects

4.1 Triggering Investigations on Illicit Enrichment

It is important for countries criminalizing illicit enrichment to consider the sources of potential cases and the sources of information for investigations. Four broad categories of sources are presented in detail in this chapter: income and asset disclosures by public officials, lifestyle checks and complaints, suspicious transaction reports from the financial sector and related businesses, and leads in other investigations. All of these can generate leads and provide helpful information.

4.1.1 Income and Asset Disclosures

Income and asset disclosures identify a public official's principal assets and liabilities.[74] In some countries, where public officials are required to disclose the value of assets and liabilities, disclosures present the official's net worth at the time of filing. Many countries extend disclosure requirements to spouses and immediate family members, and, in many systems, officials are expected to disclose at least twice during their time in office. If verified, discrepancies between an official's disclosed wealth and the wealth identified through analysis of the disclosure may be sufficient basis for further investigation into illicit enrichment.

Respondents to questionnaires and in the course of case studies stressed that public officials' financial disclosures are one of the most important tools available to investigators and prosecutors in illicit enrichment cases. In some countries, the legal provisions for illicit enrichment are embedded in the financial disclosure legislation.[75]

For the purpose of prosecuting illicit enrichment, income and asset disclosures can be used at two levels: (a) to identify illicit enrichment cases and (b) to generate evidence of illicit enrichment.

The role of disclosure systems in initiating and supporting investigations of illicit enrichment was confirmed by this study. Of the 43 jurisdictions studied that have

---

74. An upcoming study by the World Bank's Stolen Asset Recovery Initiative (StAR) will examine income and asset disclosures in detail (StAR 2012).

75. For instance, in Honduras, the Superior Court of Accounts, an independent government institution, has a duty to investigate, corroborate, and determine the existence of unlawful enrichment. And in Jamaica, the Corruption Prevention Act criminalizes passive and active corruption by public servants, embezzlement, and illicit enrichment. The CPA also requires public servants, including police officers, customs officers, revenue officials, and procurement officers, to submit a declaration of assets and liabilities.

criminalized illicit enrichment (approximately 77 percent), 34 have some form of asset disclosure regime.

However, disclosures can only be used to initiate an investigation if the disclosure has been filed. Compliance tends to be inconsistent where there are no criminal or administrative sanctions for failing to file a disclosure form, as reported by Paraguay, for instance.

Public officials should be required to provide complete and accurate information. Verification of disclosures at the time of filing may provide some assurance that public officials are meeting this requirement. However, verification systems are likely to be selective, given the number of public officials subject to disclosure requirements in most jurisdictions. In countries with administrative or criminal sanctions for failure to disclose, incomplete filing, and the filing of false information, public officials have an incentive to provide complete and accurate information. In countries where there are sanctions for submitting false information, the public official's failure to do so can be used as evidence at trial, and the incomplete or inaccurate disclosures can be used as evidence in court.

The agency responsible for managing the income and asset disclosure system should be empowered to conduct preliminary verification. If disclosures are not reviewed, they will not serve as a source of potential cases. In some countries, Jordan, for instance, the responsible agency cannot initiate an investigation until a complaint has been filed against a specific public official. That said, a cursory verification of large numbers of disclosures is unlikely to generate useful leads. A more targeted, risk-based approach is likely to be needed, concentrating attention on a few high-risk red flags.

Prosecutors and investigators should have access to disclosures at the early stages of their investigations. In some countries, such as Argentina, financial information is presented in annexes, but asset declarations are deemed public records. Parties interested in viewing or obtaining a copy of the declaration may submit a written request to the anticorruption office for access to some information, depending on the sensitivity. This information remains fully accessible by judicial authorities, the National Commission of Public Ethics, or the Fiscal de Control Administrativo (in the latter case, only upon decision by the Ministry of Justice and Human Rights with notice given to the investigated individual). In terms of initiating investigations, Argentine law authorizes the commencement of an investigation by the National Commission of Public Ethics (and by extension the anticorruption office) for both illicit enrichment and violations of the asset disclosure and conflict of interest regime. However, less than 4 percent of illicit enrichment cases in Argentina are initiated through the analysis of income and asset disclosure forms.[76]

---

76. According to research during the course of this study, most illicit enrichment cases in Argentina are initiated through a combination of leads in other cases, media coverage, internal audits, and complaints lodged by whistle-blowers and nongovernmental organizations.

In Honduras, the Superior Court of Accounts (Tribunal Supremo de Cuentas) is given complete access to financial statements and bank accounts of civil servants and their relatives during its investigations of illicit enrichment.

4.1.2 Lifestyle Checks and Complaints

Lifestyle checks are inquiries into whether the lifestyle of a public official is manifestly out of proportion to his or her known income. They are undertaken by examining the assets, activities, and expenditures of a public official. These may include a valuation of immovable property and vehicles, verification of income, stocks, nature of schools attended by children, loan and tax payments, travel, extravagant parties, and other expenditures. Lifestyle checks may also include reputational and family background checks, which are a useful starting point and subject to corroboration. To avoid abuse, standard operating procedures may be developed on how to run lifestyle checks.

Prior to investigations, a useful source of lifestyle checks and an aid to detecting illicit enrichment are complaints or allegations from members of the civil society, nongovernmental organizations (NGOs) specializing in anticorruption, the media, and whistle-blowers. The United Nations Convention against Corruption (UNCAC) under Article 33 directs state parties to consider "appropriate measures to provide protection against any unjustified treatment for any person who reports in good faith and on reasonable grounds to the competent authorities any facts concerning offenses established in accordance with this convention." The intention is to create an environment in which individuals can provide information that generates or supports investigations.

Most countries have mechanisms in place to lodge a complaint. However, few have mechanisms to protect the anonymity of a whistle-blower whose identity is revealed. In some countries, generally no action is taken on anonymous and pseudonymous complaints unless they contain specific allegations and disclose vital information, which can help in the investigation of the act in question. An environment conducive to NGO and media participation allows the free participation of the press and the free flow of information.

Some countries have adopted a cautious approach seeking to protect officials from potentially frivolous accusations. Some systems discourage frivolous accusations by the threat of sanctions. In Romania, for instance, untrue statements or "deceitful evidence" in complaints are subject to sanctions. Other countries even require a financial surety to lodge a complaint.

This approach may protect the privacy of public officials, but it may also discourage many legitimate complaints that could serve as the basis for successful prosecutions. According to responses to the questionnaire, Lebanon is currently reviewing the requirement for individuals filing a complaint to deposit a substantial bank guarantee (for example, US$18,000) for precisely these reasons. While these issues are more appropriately left to whistle-blower protection laws and not dealt with in greater detail in this study, they should be considered in implementing illicit enrichment laws, as they may have an impact on the detection of illicit enrichment.

4.1.3 Suspicious Transaction Reports

First, although the Financial Access Task Force (FATF)—the international standard-setter for anti-money-laundering (AML) policies—does not consider illicit enrichment a predicate offense for money laundering, the UNCAC considers it a nonmandatory corruption offense. As corruption is one of the predicate offenses of an effective AML regime, it may be argued on this basis that illicit enrichment is implicitly a predicate offense. The AML tools aim to prevent and detect the proceeds of crime.

Although illicit enrichment may not always be detected through banking assets, the financial sector can play an important role in detecting cases of illicit enrichment, since FATF standards require financial institutions and designated nonfinancial businesses and professions to implement "customer due diligence" as a basic AML requirement.

Where the activity of the customer account differs from the expected, financial institutions are required to file a suspicious transaction report (STR) with the country's financial intelligence unit (FIU) in respect of predicate offenses recognized by that jurisdiction. The FIU will analyze the STR and may refer the case to the prosecutor or law enforcement agencies if sufficient grounds are found for prosecuting money laundering or related offenses. In cases where the information before a prosecutor fails to establish all the elements of a corruption or economic crime, the STR may be useful for an illicit enrichment prosecution. Suspicious transaction reports may also be helpful in supporting investigations involving financial transactions held by politically exposed persons, or individuals who are or have been entrusted with prominent public functions in a foreign country, as defined by the FATF.[77]

4.1.4 Other Investigations

Frequently, during an inquiry or in the process of investigating other cases, investigators might come across information suggesting that illicit enrichment has taken place. While this is the case with most forms of financial investigation, this is particularly notable in the case of illicit enrichment, which in some countries can be prosecuted when other crimes cannot be. For example, in República Bolivariana de Venezuela, the illicit enrichment provision states that the offense may be prosecuted "provided that it does not constitute another crime."[78] These investigations are also initiated by anticorruption and

---

77. The FATF is expected to amend this definition to include domestic politically exposed persons.

78. See República Bolivariana de Venezuela, Anti-Corruption Law, Article 73, which states, "Any public servant who in the performance of his duties obtains an increase in his net worth that is disproportionate in comparison to his income and that he cannot justify, upon being requested so to do and provided that it does not constitute another crime, shall be punished by a prison term of between three (3) and ten (10) years. The same penalty shall apply to third parties who intervene to cover up such unjustified increases in net worth."

FIGURE 4.1 Triggers of Illicit Enrichment Investigations in India

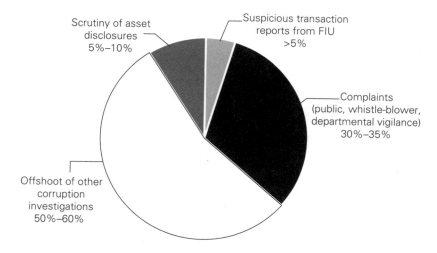

Scrutiny of asset disclosures 5%–10%

Suspicious transaction reports from FIU >5%

Complaints (public, whistle-blower, departmental vigilance) 30%–35%

Offshoot of other corruption investigations 50%–60%

Source: Information received during the course of this study from the authorities at the Central Bureau of Investigations in India.

other officers and may be based on information received through sources that do not want to come forward. Figure 4.1 shows the origins of illicit enrichment investigations in India.

4.2 Strengthening Investigations on Illicit Enrichment

4.2.1 Domestic Coordination

Broadly speaking, there are two institutional models for identifying, investigating, and prosecuting illicit enrichment (and corruption offenses more generally). In the first, illicit enrichment is subject to the same criminal procedure as any other offense. The investigation and prosecution functions are institutionally separate. Investigators and prosecutors may specialize in corruption cases, but the institutional arrangements are basically the same as for any other crime, meaning that special arrangements are not put in place for illicit enrichment. This model is found in both civil and common law jurisdictions. In the second, anticorruption legislation designates an ad hoc institution or individual to carry out the investigative or prosecutorial mandate for illicit enrichment. This approach is found mainly in common law jurisdictions.[79]

---

79. In Malawi, the Anti-Corruption Bureau is charged with sole responsibility for investigating illicit enrichment, which has to be carried out by "the director, the deputy director, or any officer of the bureau authorized in writing by the director." Similarly, in India, illicit enrichment "shall not be investigated without the order of a police officer not below the rank of a superintendent of police." Prevention of Corruption Act of 1988, Section 17(c).

Both models present the challenge of coordination, as the investigation and prosecution of illicit enrichment require a large number of institutions to exchange information and coordinate beyond investigators and prosecutors. Indeed, successful prosecution of illicit enrichment may require coordination among institutions responsible for managing income and asset disclosures (sometimes placed in an anticorruption agency), the FIU, tax authorities, property and other registries, and the entity responsible for international cooperation.

4.2.2 Building a Financial Profile

Building a solid case demonstrating a discrepancy in assets requires investigators to construct a financial profile of the public official from a starting point in time up to the point where the alleged illicit enrichment is identified. The financial profile will demonstrate what the official owns, owes, earns from legitimate sources of income, and spends over a period of time. Forensic accountants have developed various techniques for constructing and presenting financial profiles, the net worth analysis[80] being one of the most commonly used and long recognized by courts.[81] Other techniques focus on elements of the financial profile, such as expenditures relative to known income or bank deposits, to identify unknown sources of funds.

Selecting the appropriate starting point or baseline for the financial profile is critical. This starting point may be the official's entry in office or employment. If the official has been employed for a long time, a more recent date may be chosen. In either case, the profile requires documentation and other evidence regarding the official's assets and liabilities. Without a reliable baseline, it will be impossible to determine whether subsequent receipts and payments are legitimate or not. Caution should be exercised to avoid unduly narrow investigations, which might disregard key assets. Conducting checks for overly lengthy periods may present similar challenges. For example, countries where stability of currency is a concern may have difficulty assessing the value of properties acquired over a lengthy period.

As demonstrated by the approach in some states, it may be helpful for an illicit enrichment provision to extend for a reasonable period beyond a public official's term of office, so that any corrupt benefits received during this period can be included in the prosecution (see chapter 2). Such a provision can be supplemented by administrative instructions that give guidance to the prosecution on how to exercise discretion in prosecuting illicit enrichment.

A declaration of assets, a loan application, or tax information will usually provide basic information for a baseline financial profile. This information will have to be verified. Assets may include accounts in various banks, securities or options in public and private corporations, insurance policies and other financial instruments, movable property

---

80. Drawn from U.S. Internal Revenue Service, Department of Treasury (1994). For additional analysis of the application of these methods, see Botha (2009).
81. The U.S. Supreme Court recognized net worth analysis as prima facie evidence of a crime in 1954 in *Holland v. United States*, 348 US 121, 75 S. St 127.

(boat, plane) and real estate, and high-value items such as antiques, art, and jewelry. The acquisition of assets has to be valued at the purchase price (the cost at the time they were acquired); the disposal of assets has to be at the sale price. Liabilities may include loans and mortgages, some of which may not be through formal financial institutions. The investigator also has to identify all legitimate sources of income and track expenditures.

Because illicit enrichment criminalizes merely the existence of a significant increase in a public official's assets without a viable explanation, the prosecution therefore does not have to demonstrate or link the assets to any underlying criminal act. This is the major advantage of the criminalization of illicit enrichment from a prosecutorial perspective.

4.2.3 Tools and Skills to Facilitate Investigations

Most of these requirements are not specific to investigations related to illicit enrichment. They are obviously a prerequisite for any effective investigation on financial crimes. However, they are of special interest when investigating or prosecuting illicit enrichment due to the complexity of the investigations. Showing an increase in assets during a period of time is not such an easy task, and many challenges will occur during the course of the investigation.

In order to compile all relevant information, investigators will need to have access to a wide range of data sources and registries. These will include public property and vehicle registries, bank account records, and records of financial institutions. Additional information may have to be collected through interviews with third parties familiar with the official's financial affairs, including accountants and lawyers. On-site inspections may be needed to identify assets that are not documented.

Since it is often impossible to track all income and expenditures, the investigator will have to make some assumptions and draw inferences. There are particular challenges in determining the amount of cash on hand—money not deposited with financial institutions—and expenditures. The amount of cash on hand may have to be inferred from other financial records, and expenditures will often have to be estimated on the basis of assumptions regarding a reasonable cost of living. Where businesses are involved, a forensic accountant may have to construct a profile and compare key characteristics of the business activities with those of comparable enterprises. The courts will subsequently have to determine whether these inferences and assumptions are convincing.

Beyond the financial profile and the evidence of disproportion between legitimate income and growth in net worth, expenditures, or bank deposits, the prosecutor or investigative magistrate may be able to draw other inferences from the circumstances of the case. For instance, the prosecution may be able to point to measures taken by the official to conceal the funds. The prosecution or magistrate may also be able to point to leads and theories regarding the corrupt conduct that generated the alleged illicit enrichment, even if these cannot be proven to the requisite standard.

It is also important to investigate discreetly and to verify the suspect's personal and familial particulars. It may be useful in this respect to draw up a list of close family and associates in whose names key assets may be held or who may be in a position to lend assistance in the concealment of assets.

Provisions will need to be put in place for the preservation of assets pending disposal of the illicit enrichment case. This may include powers to obtain orders at any time to freeze and seize the property in possession of an accused, any relative, any associate, or any person on his behalf. Another alternative is to prohibit by statute the transfer of property subject to prosecution once an investigation has been initiated, as in Pakistan.[82] In order to strengthen the efficiency and effectiveness of investigations, the investigating team may use the services of document experts and notaries to prove forgeries or antedated documentation of false inheritance. Cyber forensics experts may also be useful in a variety of ways, including analyzing hard disks, cracking passwords to unearth proof of beneficial ownership, and tracking foreign remittances and dematerialized accounts. In addition, forensic accountants on the team may help to disprove false claims of income by the associates as well as detect the use of corporate vehicles. From an early stage, it will be helpful to have valuators on hand who can immediately assist with the valuation of any assets subject to an illicit enrichment investigation.

4.3 Process and Interaction with the Public Official during the Investigation

4.3.1 Stages of the Procedure

An illicit enrichment case is initiated by an investigation and is followed by prosecution through the different stages outlined in chapter 2 and in figure 2.1.

Once sufficient evidence has been gathered through investigation, different jurisdictions take different approaches. On the one hand, evidence may be presented to allow the public official to provide a reasonable explanation; on the other hand, a case may be instituted immediately to allow the official to provide an explanation in court.

Regarding the sequence of events, once the investigation has revealed the existence of disproportionate assets and the public servant has failed to account or explain such

---

82. Section 23 of the National Accountability Ordinance in Pakistan, reads, "(a) Notwithstanding anything contained in any other law for the time being in force after the chairman [of the] NAB [National Accountability Bureau] has initiated investigation into the offenses under this ordinance, alleged to have been committed by an accused person, such person or any relative or associate of such person, or any other person on his behalf, shall not transfer by any means whatsoever, create a charge on any movable or immovable property owned by him or in his possession, while the inquiry, investigation, or proceedings are pending before the NAB or the Accountability Court; and any transfer of any right, title, or interest or creation of a charge on such property shall be void. (b) Any person who transfers or creates a charge on property in contravention of subsection (a) shall be punishable with rigorous imprisonment for a term, which may extend to three years, and shall also be liable to a fine not exceeding the value of the property involved."

excess, the offense becomes complete. This does not mean that a charge cannot be framed until the public servant fails to explain the excess or surplus, as this exercise can be completed only in the trial.[83] In other words, a public servant may be charged with illicit enrichment before failing to provide a reasonable explanation at trial.

In India, after all evidence has been collected, the investigating officer is not legally bound to ask a suspect to account for the excess of the assets over the known sources of income, as to do so would elevate him to the position of an enquiry officer or a judge.[84] The investigating officer is only required to collect material to find out whether the alleged offense appears to have been committed and may, in the course of the investigation, examine the accused. Indeed, fair investigation requires that the accused should not be kept in the dark, especially if he is willing to cooperate.

In Pakistan, a standard operating procedure established in 2006 established that, upon receipt of a complaint and before initiating an inquiry, the accused would be given an opportunity to explain his assets to save him the embarrassment of a formal inquiry if he is able to justify them.

In rebutting the prosecution's case, the accused may demonstrate that the increase in net worth, expenditures, or bank deposits originated from legitimate sources. Substantiated explanations may include inheritance of assets, lottery or gambling winnings, employment outside the public sector, as well as proceeds from investments, business interests, or income-generating activities. Occasionally, an illicit enrichment case has turned on the legitimacy of the source of income. In the *Alsogaray* case in Argentina, for example, the accused sought to justify a portion of the increase in her fortune by demonstrating that she regularly received informal allowances from the Argentine Intelligence Agency that were paid to her as "salary bonus." While the court accepted the fact that the allowances were paid regularly and ordered the opening of a formal criminal investigation over such facts, it ultimately held that these payments were not legitimate.

In many cases, even if the public official's enrichment is legally explained, he or she may still remain liable for other offenses (box 4.1).

4.4 Enforcing Illicit Enrichment: The Challenges

The most significant challenge in investigating and prosecuting illicit enrichment cases is the collection of evidence. This section presents a few examples of challenges that the investigators and prosecutors will face when charging a public official for illicit

---

83. *State by Central Bureau of Investigation v. Shri S. Bangarappa* (2000), INSC 578 (20 November 2000); *K. Veeraswami v. Union of India* (1991), (3) SCC 655; *State of Maharashtra v. Ishwar Pirazji Kalpatri* (1996), 1 SCC 542, 1996 AIR SCW 15, AIR 1996 SC 722, 1996 Cri LJ 1127.
84. *State of Maharashtra v. Wasudeo Ramchandra Kaidalwar* (1981), 3 SCR 675.

- *False declarations in financial disclosures.* In most countries that have this system in place, officials who omit or provide false information in their financial disclosures are subject to prosecution.

- *Unauthorized employment and gifts.* Public administrations often prohibit public officials from taking paid employment or receiving gifts.

- *Tax offenses.* As with any other taxpayer, public officials who have not declared income to the tax authorities may be liable to prosecution for tax evasion. Again, in the United States the authorities may prosecute a 26 U.S.C. 2601, Section 7201, offense by proving three elements: the existence of a tax deficiency, an affirmative act constituting an evasion or attempted evasion of the tax, and willfulness. The techniques employed in investigating illicit enrichment are directly applicable to the presentation of evidence in tax evasion cases.

- *Foreign accounts holding.* Some countries—notably Nigeria and more recently Kenya—prohibit public officials from holding foreign bank accounts. Others, such as China, require these accounts to be authorized. Failure to comply with these requirements can lead to prosecution. Foreign exchange control also applies to public officials in other countries, such as Tunisia.

enrichment. Many of these are not specific to illicit enrichment but are encountered in most financial investigations.

4.4.1 Access to Registries and Relevant Databases

In many countries, up-to-date searchable databases do not exist and therefore cannot be used to identify assets. For example, in response to the questionnaire, Paraguay cited the lack of actualized databases for land titles as a major obstacle to investigations. In other countries, data are dispersed among numerous, independent registries. Some countries have invested heavily in information systems in an effort to consolidate information. This is the case in Pakistan, where a central database, tied to a national identification card, stores information, including data from property and other registries. Chile has a similar facility, with online access to property registries, licensing information, and tax records.

The same impediment arises for the identification of bank accounts. In many countries, the lack of a centralized database or efficient tools for tracing assets may hinder the ability to have a comprehensive view of the assets held domestically by a public official.

Investigators generally have to undertake legal proceedings to gain access to evidence. This may entail court authorization for the release of tax records, income and asset disclosures, financial records, as well as searches and seizure of documents. In some cases, tax returns are filed on fictitious returns as an advance way of preparing a legitimate explanation for the illicit funds. Verifying gift tax returns and foreign bank returns are useful means of disproving potential false claims of gifts. In this respect, it is useful to scrutinize closely the tax returns of the suspect and any close family or associates in order to detect any belated returns made as an afterthought to cover the illicit enrichment.

4.4.2 Cash Economies and Valuation of Properties

Financial investigations are particularly difficult in countries with a substantial cash economy. In these countries, it is not unusual for individuals to hold substantial amounts of cash and to make large payments outside of the banking system. For example, in many Middle Eastern and South Asian jurisdictions, some transactions, including international transfers for trade and migrants' remittances, are channeled through informal *hawala* networks and simply go unrecorded for official purposes. Where transactions take place in cash, they may be difficult, if not impossible, to trace.

In certain cases, the actual value of real estate properties may be manipulated by over-valuing or undervaluing property followed by a succession of sales and purchases. This practice consists of buying or selling a property at a price above or below its market value, often by people who are related. In other cases, the immovable properties that are purchased by corrupt officers are highly undervalued and cannot be challenged because the calculation of disproportion usually considers the registered value.

To address the problem of valuation, and to safeguard against potential challenges by the suspect, it may be beneficial for investigators and prosecutors to take a conservative valuation of properties, which is often the registration value at the time of acquisition. Where it is allowed by a particular jurisdiction, the use of special investigative techniques may prove to be highly valuable. For example, the use of visual technology may add value to the evidence, as the judge often cannot see the physical assets in person. It may also be very helpful to take evidence from multiple sources to rebut evidence that does not leave a paper trail, such as agriculture income.

4.4.3 The Use of Third Parties

Preparation of an accurate financial profile is further complicated by the use of third parties, front entities, and straw men to disguise the ownership of assets. Several countries cite the use of third parties as one of the principal obstacles to prosecuting illicit enrichment. Identifying assets held in the name of associates and third parties can be extremely difficult for investigators, especially where evidence is layered through a series of corporate vehicles in multiple jurisdictions.[85]

---

85. A recent StAR publication highlights the difficulties faced by investigators in tracing corrupt funds where the beneficial ownership of assets is obscured by the abuse of corporate vehicles (van der Does de Willebois et al. 2011).

> **BOX 4.2   The *Benamis* in India**
>
> For transactions made in the name of another person, or *benami*, the jurisprudence is mixed. In *K. Ponnuswamy v. State of Tamil Nadu by Inspector of Police*, the court interpreted the law broadly to allow an inference of ownership over assets held by the son of the accused, even without any direct evidence supporting this inference. However, the court tempered the holding by asserting that, had the son of the accused been employed during the period, this inference would not have been permitted without corroborating evidence.
>
> The court further restricted its interpretation in *Chennai v. Inbasagaran*, when it held that a spouse's assertion of ownership over large sums of cash found in the home of the accused, when supported by evidence, could not be counted against the total assets of the accused. The current rule therefore holds that *benami* transactions can be inferred unless the asset holder demonstrates ownership with both testimony and evidence. For example, according to jurisprudence, those responsible for *benami* transactions may be held liable under the catch-all abetment provision that includes abetting nonenumerated criminal acts.

Other challenges encountered by investigators may be culturally specific. For example, in some cultures, such as in India, married adult children often continue living in the same household as their parents and all resources and salaries may be held in a common account. In such a situation, segregating incomes in a family of multiple earners can prove to be extremely difficult. Family trusts are also often created, which makes it difficult to detect the enrichment. In addition, it may be difficult to disprove explanations offered by a suspect who may justify the enrichment in terms of a loan, false inheritance, or gift, particularly where prosecution takes place long after the initial enrichment.

There are also legal challenges. Family members, straw men, and front entities may be able to demonstrate legal ownership of assets and claim that these assets are not a legitimate target of investigation. Legislation has sought to address this problem by including in the calculation of net worth assets held by family members and, in some countries, possible associates of public officials (box 4.2 describes the *benami* jurisprudence in India).

Some illicit enrichment provisions seek to punish and deter accomplices that help public officials to conceal the proceeds of corruption by including them within the scope of the illicit enrichment law. However, most countries deal with the issue of third parties through specific legislation concerning accomplice or accessory liability or money laundering. This is the same approach taken by the UNCAC, which, according to which Article 27(1), requires state parties to take legislative and other measures as may be necessary to establish as a criminal offense the participation in any capacity, such as an accomplice, assistant, or instigator, in an offense established under the convention.

4.4.4 Original Solutions to Overcome Challenges

In order to address practical challenges in investigating and prosecuting illicit enrichment, states may consider plea bargaining to be a means of recovering illicit wealth. In Pakistan, an accused facing an investigation or prosecution for illicit enrichment is allowed to volunteer to return the illicit wealth and any gains derived from it. If the National Accountability Bureau accepts his offer, the suspect is discharged from liability and not deemed to be convicted. After authorization of investigation, while the trial or appeal is pending, the suspect or accused may apply for a plea bargain by making an offer for his liability, which, if accepted by the National Accountability Bureau, is referred to court for approval. This approach facilitates the expeditious disposal of a case, the recovery of proceeds of corruption, and the disqualification from office, while avoiding practical challenges in enforcing illicit enrichment.[86]

Where investigations suggest an international element to the case, experience has shown that it is useful to check immigration and customs records for ascertaining and proving foreign travels. The use of relevant networks, such as the Egmont Group of Financial Intelligence Units, the StAR–International Criminal Police Organization (INTERPOL) Focal Point Initiative Database, and AML agencies, can be helpful in providing informal assistance to the investigation. It is also beneficial for countries to strive to enter into more bilateral treaties on mutual legal assistance and extradition, which are less restrictive with regard to the use to which assistance can be directed.

4.5 Assessing the Effectiveness of an Illicit Enrichment Regime

4.5.1 Penalties and Forfeiture

As with most crimes, states can impose various penalties for a conviction for illicit enrichment, but penalties should be aligned with the objectives of legislation. Four broad objectives have been identified: (a) to restore to the state losses that have occurred through corruption; (b) to punish officials who engage in illicit enrichment; (c) to prevent them from benefiting from ill-gotten gains, signaling through prosecution that crime does not pay, thereby providing an effective deterrence; and (d) to incapacitate them through dismissal or prison sentences.

These objectives are achieved through a combination of fines, incarceration, and forfeiture of the proceeds of the crime. Lastly, in addition to incarceration, public officials may also be subject to administrative and civil sanctions, which include termination of employment, prohibition from holding elected office, and restrictions on the right to

---

86. Pakistan National Accountability Ordinance, Sections 25(a) and 25(b).

stand for office and to vote. These provide a level of incapacitation, as the official is prevented from committing further wrongdoing.

In practice, states have adopted two approaches in stipulating the applicable penalty for illicit enrichment: it either is specified in the illicit enrichment provision or is listed in the penalties common to the anticorruption crimes contained in an act. In the latter case, an act containing anticorruption provisions would not distinguish the penalties for illicit enrichment from those for other corruption offenses.

Most countries rely on a combination of economic sanctions and incarceration, with some requiring incarceration only where the official does not pay the economic penalty. Some countries provide for the recovery of assets accumulated within the period of illicit enrichment. As said earlier, when defining the scope of the study, some jurisdictions, such as Chile, the Philippines, or Romania, do not provide for incarceration as a penalty for the offense, relying entirely on economic penalties. Other countries do not include economic penalties in their illicit enrichment law, providing only for periods of incarceration. However, some of these countries have criminal forfeiture regimes that theoretically may be applied following conviction.

Across the jurisdictions that provide for incarceration, prison terms are set within a range of a minimum of 14 days to a maximum of 12 years, with most countries falling in the range of between two to five years. For example, the required term of imprisonment in India may be for a term of one to seven years, and the convict is liable to a fine. Most countries leave the sentencing to the full discretion of the court. However, some countries have set the graduated penalties based on the absolute amount found to be the product of illicit enrichment. Panama, for instance, has two applicable ranges: three to six years if convicted and five to 12 years if the illicit wealth exceeds US$100,000.

Fines tend to be structured differently depending on the circumstances of each case and jurisdiction. At times, they are equivalent in value to confiscating the illicit enrichment proceeds, with an additional amount as a punitive measure. In Ecuador, the fine is double the amount of illicit enrichment. Some set graduated fines in absolute amounts: in Madagascar, the amount is approximately US$5,000 to US$20,000; in Colombia, the fine is up to approximately US$1,000 complemented by one to eight years of jail time. When imposing a fine in India, in contrast, the court is directed to consider the pecuniary resources or property for which the accused person is unable to account satisfactorily.

Forfeiture of the proceeds of illicit enrichment is conviction based. In the cases reviewed, two approaches have been taken. In the first, assets subjected to confiscation have had a direct link to the offense—that is, they cannot be reasonably explained. This was the approach adopted in the Mzumara case in Malawi.[87] Another approach involves confiscating property amounting to the difference between the legitimate income and the overall assets. This is the approach adopted in Argentina. The ill-gotten proceeds are

---

87. Described in box 1.1. *State v. Mzumar,* Criminal Case no. 47 of 2010.

targeted based on the assessment of illicit enrichment. The amounts recovered can be substantial. In India, about US$10 million has been recovered through illicit enrichment investigations, according to the authorities. Argentina has recovered assets in only one case, totaling US$650,000 and applied fines in other cases. In Hong Kong SAR, China, assets have been recovered in 24 instances, worth HK$47,467,912 (US$6,085,630).

Trends have not yet emerged to show whether confiscation and fines are taken into account by the courts in mitigation of a sentence. In fact, persons convicted of illicit enrichment in Argentina routinely incur more than one type of penalty. This is also demonstrated by the *Alsogaray* case described in box 4.3.

The appropriate balance between the penalties for illicit enrichment will depend on the legislators' objectives. Where the primary objective is to address the underlying economic—acquisitive—motivation for the corrupt conduct, it would be appropriate to give greater weight to restitution, forfeiture, and fines, requiring these sanctions in all instances of the crime.

BOX 4.3   The Alsogaray Case in Argentina

The accused, María Julia Alsogaray, was in public service from 1985 until 1999 when she was the minister of natural resources and human environment in Argentina. The proceedings against her were triggered by a complaint filed by an individual who cited the "explosive economic glitz" in which she was living and her "sudden change of image" since assuming her functions working for the government.

In laying out its case, the prosecution collected all documents, reports, and relevant testimony and made a comparative chart demonstrating the accumulation of her assets for the years 1988 to 1996. According to the court, the significant increase in the assets of the accused was demonstrated by a comparison of her assets when she assumed public office (consisting of one real estate property, two automobiles, assets worth about US$8,000, and stocks in companies), with those added during the course of her public functions (consisting of five real estate properties, a garage, a canopy, two real estate properties in New York, four automobiles, and an increase in her stocks). In conclusion, the court found that Alsogaray had illegally enriched herself in the sum of US$500,000 or Arg$622,000.

The accused was then required to provide a detailed justification of her wealth. In her defense, Alsogaray declared that some of her unexplained income was on account of fees for her professional activity in various companies, some was given to her by her former husband, and some consisted of donations received from her father. The court was not convinced by her explanation and found no justification for her enrichment. Consequently, she was convicted, sentenced to three years imprisonment, barred from public office for a period of six years, and ordered to pay compensation in the amount of US$500,000 (Arg$622,000).

Source: Maria J. Alsogaray, Cámara Nacional de Casación Penal (National Chamber of Criminal Appeals), 9 June 2005.

However, legislators may consider that the forfeiture of the proceeds of corruption and additional economic sanctions may not offer adequate or sufficient deterrence and may not satisfy public expectations regarding the punishment of corrupt officials.

Provisions for incarceration in high-profile cases, where there is significant damage to the public interest owing to the scale and nature of the corruption, may be used to ensure that the punishment is proportionate to the crime.

4.5.2 Performance

Experience in the prosecution of illicit enrichment can be broken into three broad categories of jurisdictions: first, those jurisdictions that have not yet prosecuted cases or have experience in only a few cases; second, countries that have prosecuted illicit enrichment over an extended period of time but use the illicit enrichment offense sparingly; and third, countries that have prosecuted illicit enrichment over an extended period of time and use the illicit enrichment offense frequently.

Countries that have not yet prosecuted cases include countries that have only recently criminalized illicit enrichment and countries that criminalized illicit enrichment some time ago but have only recently begun to pursue cases actively. Malawi is an example of the latter group. Illicit enrichment was criminalized in 1994, but prosecutions have only been brought in the last three years. Prosecutors have recently secured three convictions for modest cases in the lower courts. One of these was tested in the appeals courts, and the sentence was reduced. The limited track record of successful prosecutions and limited case law are a source of uncertainty and may discourage prosecutors from initiating further cases. In this context, further development of illicit enrichment cases will require support from prosecution authorities to address potential risks, investments in capacity, and favorable judgments from the courts.

Some countries have prosecuted illicit enrichment over an extended period, but still use the offense sparingly. Argentina falls into this category. Illicit enrichment was criminalized in 1964, but the offense was not used until 1994, when a constitutional amendment provided support for the underlying concept and encouraged the authorities to initiate prosecutions. Over the decade 2000 to 2009, 39 cases of illicit enrichment were prosecuted, with 29 convictions.

Illicit enrichment in Argentina represents approximately one in eight complaints relating to corruption crimes, trailing behind embezzlement and bribery. The proportion of illicit enrichment offenses that go to trial after complaints are lodged or investigations are opened is significantly lower than complaints and investigations opened for bribery and embezzlement individually.

In Argentina, only 14 out of every 100 complaints are illicit enrichment cases (table 4.1). Further, only 6.3 trials are illicit enrichment cases. However, the conviction rate is significantly higher for illicit enrichment, with a conviction in 14 percent of corruption cases brought to trial. This is largely due to the ability of prosecutors to identify cases that are likely to be successful in court, and interviews with those suspected of illicit enrichment are often able to identify a legitimate source of increase in wealth. In response to the questionnaires, El Salvador and Panama each reported that they have brought only one case, neither of which has yet resulted in a conviction.

TABLE 4.1	Investigation, Prosecution, and Conviction of Illicit Enrichment and Other Corruption Offenses in Argentina, 2000–09 *% of cases*		
Offense	Complaint	Trial	Conviction
Bribery	29.0	24.6	26.2
Embezzlement	52.6	65.8	56.3
Conflict of interests	4.0	3.4	3.4
Illicit enrichment	14.4	6.3	14.1
Total crimes	100.0	100.0	100.0

Source: Information provided by the Anti-Corruption Office of Argentina in 2010.

The third category of jurisdictions includes countries that have prosecuted illicit enrichment over an extended period of time and still use the illicit enrichment offense frequently. In these jurisdictions, illicit enrichment is presented as a key tool in combating corruption, for instance, in Bangladesh, India, and Pakistan. In Pakistan, since the National Accountability Ordinance was enacted in 1999, 280 cases of illicit enrichment have been filed before the courts. Of these, 127 ended in convictions, 52 ended in acquittals, and 25 were withdrawn (table 4.2). This adds up to a 62.25 percent conviction rate of completed illicit enrichment cases.

TABLE 4.2	Status of Illicit Enrichment Cases in Pakistan, 1999–2011
Status	Number of cases
Filed in the courts	280
Conviction	127
Acquittal	52
Withdrawn	25
Under progress	76

Source: Information provided by the National Accountability Bureau of Pakistan in 2010.

In Hong Kong SAR, China, between 1971 and 1994, the case-based conviction rate for illicit enrichment was 64.7 percent. Notwithstanding the impressive conviction rate for illicit enrichment, some national authorities report that prosecutors tend to consider illicit enrichment as an offense of last resort; when they do investigate and prosecute it, they often do so alongside other corruption offenses. This is partly because illicit enrichment is considered difficult to investigate, requiring the compilation of a substantial amount of data and accounting expertise.

The authorities in Hong Kong SAR, China, reported that they have preferred measures other than illicit enrichment prosecutions since 1994. This is because the offense of misconduct in public office is used for civil servants who have acted alone in abusing their office for personal gain and for public sector corruption offenses under the Prevention of Bribery Ordinance. This experience is symptomatic of the use of illicit enrichment to tackle rampant corruption in public sectors, such as the police or other exposed administrations. The offense has been extensively used in the past to restrain the phenomenon, and the deterrence effect is more prevalent, according to the authorities.

In jurisdictions frequently prosecuting the offense, illicit enrichment is seen as a preferred offense for prosecuting corruption. Several factors explain this approach. The first relates to the legal context. Illicit enrichment has a successful track record of prosecution in India and the support of courts. As the courts are familiar with the offense, they are generally willing to provide search warrants for investigators to collect physical and documentary evidence at an early stage of investigations and have settled potential constitutional issues, meaning that convictions and sentences are less likely to be overturned on these grounds on appeal. Consequently, illicit enrichment prosecution is seen as a low-risk case for prosecutors. The institutional framework is also favorable. In both India and Pakistan, public servants are required to file income and asset declarations and report on the acquisition of assets above a certain threshold. Courts have generally viewed failure to report as undermining claims from the defense regarding the legitimate origin of assets. Furthermore, the majority of public servants tend to remain in the public service for their entire career, and it is unusual to find mid-career entrants other than at the political level. This makes it considerably easier to track public servants' accumulation of assets and to signal significant changes that may warrant further investigation.

4.6 Observations

The use of illicit enrichment as an offense is most effective when it is implemented as part of a broader anticorruption strategy and where systems are in place to facilitate the identification of potential cases and generate the information needed to support investigations. Therefore, resources need to be put in place at all levels to allow the detection, tracking, and preservation of the evidence and proceeds of illicit enrichment. For instance, an effective income and asset disclosure system is a valuable support for the investigation and prosecution of illicit enrichment. In countries that have decided to criminalize this offense, consideration should be given to the design of the income and asset disclosure system and the means by which the disclosure agency interacts with agencies responsible for investigation and prosecution.[88]

---

88. Further information on the design and management of income and asset disclosure systems is presented in StAR (2012). See also Greenberg et al. (2010).

An effective income and asset disclosure system should be complemented by mechanisms for lifestyle checks, internal audits, whistle-blower protection laws, and the reporting of suspicious transactions to the financial intelligence unit.

Effective communication between investigators and prosecutors is also critical. This is as true of illicit enrichment as it is of any criminal procedure. Equally important is the existence of and access to financial records and property registries. Without such information, it is difficult for investigators to prepare a financial profile of suspects or to generate evidence of illicit enrichment. Access to income and asset disclosures of public officials in particular, but also tax returns and loan applications, can greatly facilitate the development of an appropriate baseline for investigating illicit enrichment. Law enforcement agencies will need to have financial analysts who are able to analyze this information and generate evidence that can be interpreted by nonspecialists in court. It is therefore imperative that one consider the institution that is best positioned to investigate and prosecute illicit enrichment and to accord it the necessary powers to do so.

In their fight against corruption, prosecutors tend to pursue trials and the criminal offenses that are most likely to be successful in court and least likely to be overturned on appeal. Risks of an adverse outcome will be minimized where courts are familiar with illicit enrichment cases and are prepared to support investigations by, for instance, facilitating search warrants and access to restricted information and where there is extensive jurisprudence to guide the courts on potential challenges from the defense or on appeal.

These factors suggest that there is a powerful feedback loop, where successful prosecutions will tend to encourage and facilitate further use of illicit enrichment as a prosecutable offense. In a positive feedback loop, successful prosecutions will help to develop the experience of investigators, prosecutors, and the courts, and successful prosecutions will develop case law on illicit enrichment and resolve legal challenges for appeal.

5. International Cooperation

Corrupt officials, like many other criminals, may transfer the proceeds of their crime abroad and hold accounts in foreign jurisdictions so as to evade detection and more easily enjoy their ill-gotten gains. This makes international legal cooperation a crucial part of illicit enrichment prosecutions, particularly in high-profile cases. Although all major international corruption conventions promote enhanced international cooperation in the fight against corruption,[89] the prosecution of illicit enrichment presents specific challenges.

International cooperation includes both nonjudicial cooperation—between specialized bodies such as financial intelligence units (FIUs), anticorruption agencies, banking supervisors, and police units working upon initiative—and mutual legal assistance (MLA), which can be described as "the formal way in which countries request and provide assistance in obtaining evidence located in one country to assist in criminal investigations or proceedings in another country."[90] MLA can be requested at any point in an investigation, during trial, or for the execution of a judgment by a court in another jurisdiction. While MLA may be provided on an ad hoc basis, legal frameworks such as bilateral treaties, conventions, and memoranda of understanding are usually necessary for countries to obtain or reply to formal requests for mutual legal assistance and extradition.[91]

Article 46 of the United Nations Convention against Corruption (UNCAC) requires state parties to afford each other the widest measure of assistance in relation to the corruption offenses covered by the treaty.[92] The convention lays out the conditions and procedures that can be used to request and render assistance.[93] UNCAC state parties are expected to provide legal assistance, but they are not obligated to do so, and the convention enumerates various grounds for refusal or postponement of assistance.[94]

---

89. African Union Convention on Combating Corruption, Article 18; Organization of American States, Inter-American Convention against Corruption, Article XIV; Economic Community of West African States, Protocol on the Fight against Corruption, Article 15; United Nations Convention against Corruption, Chapter IV; Organisation for Economic Co-operation and Development Convention on Combating Bribery of Foreign Public Officials in International Business Transactions, Articles 9–10.

90. The British Home Office offers basic guidelines for getting assistance from within the United Kingdom and abroad. http://www.homeoffice.gov.uk/police/mutual-legal-assistance/.

91. ADB and OECD (2006, 1). The UNCAC, Article 46(4), has broken new ground by explicitly calling for spontaneous MLA in combating corruption.

92. UNCAC, Article 46(1).

93. UNCAC, Article 46(7).

94. UNCAC, Article 46(21)–46(26).

Grounds for refusal specifically related to illicit enrichment include dual criminality, due process, and evidentiary concerns. More often than not, the real challenge is lack of understanding and miscommunication.

5.1 Addressing Dual Criminality

Dual criminality is the requirement to demonstrate that the crime underlying the request for assistance is criminalized in both the requested and the requesting jurisdictions. A strict interpretation of dual criminality by the requested jurisdiction requires the requesting jurisdiction to demonstrate that the name and elements of the offense are the same in both jurisdictions. However, UNCAC, Article 43(2), requires that dual criminality be based on the conduct underlying the offense in question.

The absence of dual criminality is a discretionary ground for refusing MLA under the United Nations Convention on Transnational Organized Crime, which states that parties can provide MLA in the absence of dual criminality when they deem it appropriate to do so. Under UNCAC, however, a state party may deny assistance only after taking into account the purposes of the convention. In addition, following Article 46(9)(b), if the request is not for coercive action, such as searches and seizures or extradition, a state party must render the assistance in the absence of dual criminality if it is consistent with their legal system to do so.

In practice, most jurisdictions do not consider dual criminality a prerequisite for the exchange of information during an investigation. However, many do require dual criminality for coercive measures such as search and seizure, and most require it for extradition. Notwithstanding the UNCAC, some countries may in practice still consider the absence of dual criminality a discretionary ground for refusing any or all assistance.[95]

Regarding illicit enrichment, the type of assistance requested from a foreign state in order to demonstrate the offense generally focuses on bank account information, real estate possession, or company ownership. Many countries may not consider the exchange of information to be coercive.

Where both the requesting and requested jurisdictions have criminalized illicit enrichment, dual criminality requirements can be satisfied fairly easily. Officials contacted during the course of this study in Paraguay and Argentina both pointed to successes in obtaining mutual legal assistance from neighboring countries in Latin America, which have similar formulations for illicit enrichment. However, the large majority of state parties to the UNCAC have not criminalized illicit enrichment, among them all of Western Europe and North America and many of the world's financial centers. Several jurisdictions reported that requests for legal assistance in illicit enrichment cases are often delayed or refused on grounds of the absence of dual criminality when dealing with jurisdictions that do not recognize the offense.

---

95. Ibid.

Objections to illicit enrichment can at times be overcome by adopting a conduct-based approach to dual criminality. A conduct-based approach requires the requested and requesting states to "transpose the facts (but not the offense) under investigation in the requesting country to the legal system of the requested country and ask whether such facts would be considered illicit if committed there" (Schmid 2006, 45). In response to the questionnaire, Argentina reported the successful use of a conduct-based approach in MLA in an illicit enrichment case from a country not criminalizing illicit enrichment (Spain), which was able to provide assistance because the facts could be interpreted as embezzlement.

Some countries, such as Uruguay, that have not criminalized illicit enrichment have reported that they would nevertheless provide international assistance in these cases, citing, as examples, mutual assistance treaties that the country has signed and Uruguayan case law (OAS 2009b).

Other jurisdictions contacted in the course of this study indicated that they would usually apply a conduct-based approach if presented with an MLA request for an illicit enrichment case. Box 5.1 describes the reservation made by the United States to the illicit enrichment provision in the Inter-American Convention against Corruption (IACAC).

Cooperation requires flexibility and effective communication on the part of both the requesting and requested states. Requesting states have to provide extensive information on the facts of the case when drafting MLA requests, bearing in mind that illicit enrichment may be associated with a wide range of offenses in almost all countries, including corruption and economic offenses (Shams 2001, n. 75).

Informal cooperation and contacts between the authorities prior to preparing an MLA request can help to identify a possible basis for assistance and help the requesting country to focus on the relevant facts before drafting (Brun et al. 2011). The issue of dual criminality can be avoided altogether where the authorities investigate and prosecute public officials for illicit enrichment alongside other corruption offenses.

5.2 Meeting Evidentiary and Due Process Standards

MLA requests usually have to be backed with sufficient admissible evidence to enable the requested jurisdiction to meet the evidentiary threshold required by the legal system. Generally, the more intrusive the measure, the higher the evidentiary standard required. Evidentiary requirements—standards of proof, evidentiary tests, and admissibility requirements—vary among jurisdictions. Failure to meet the evidentiary requirements in the requested jurisdiction may result in the request being returned or rejected.

Evidentiary requirements can be a challenge where investigations focus only on illicit enrichment without considering the criminal conduct that generated the illicit wealth.

BOX 5.1   U.S. and International Cooperation on Illicit Enrichment

The United States expressed the following reservations regarding Article IX of the IACAC:

> (4) ILLICIT ENRICHMENT The United States of America intends to assist and cooperate with other state parties pursuant to paragraph 3 of Article IX of the convention to the extent permitted by its domestic law. The United States recognizes the importance of combating improper financial gains by public officials and has criminal statutes to deter or punish such conduct. These statutes obligate senior-level officials in the federal government to file truthful financial disclosure statements, subject to criminal penalties. They also permit prosecution of federal public officials who evade taxes on wealth that is acquired illicitly. The offense of illicit enrichment as set forth in Article IX of the convention, however, places the burden of proof on the defendant, which is inconsistent with the United States constitution and fundamental principles of the United States legal system. Therefore, the United States understands that it is not obligated to establish a new criminal offense of illicit enrichment under Article IX of the convention.

Therefore, the United States will exchange information, including information on bank records, but it will not undertake coercive actions, such as searches and seizures, on behalf of the requesting country.

However, the United States will also attempt to identify other crimes that fit the conduct so that they can provide assistance that requires coercive actions as well. Typically, the crimes that can be associated with illicit enrichment include bribery, money laundering, and other economic crimes, such as fraud. The United States may also apply tax evasion as an alternative offense in illicit enrichment cases.

Prosecutions for tax evasion require similar information as prosecutions for illicit enrichment and may use comparable investigation and analysis techniques, such as net worth analysis and income statements. This is on condition that no evidentiary restrictions are placed on the use of evidence provided.

Source: Statement of Thomas Burrows, trial attorney, Office of International Affairs, U.S. Department of Justice.

Evidence of this criminal conduct may have to be presented to provide a basis for MLA on the grounds of corruption offenses, embezzlement, money laundering, and economic crimes such as fraud, depending on the case. This underlines the importance of undertaking a broad investigation of the suspects' criminal activities. Even if the evidence of criminal conduct may not be sufficient to support a conviction for that particular offense, the suspicion may be sufficient to support MLA requests for other offenses.

In this respect, any contextual information on the suspect should be detailed in the MLA request, including public function, duration, type of duties (that is, awarding public contracts, managing public funds, supervising private entities, and so forth), and amount of assets already calculated domestically. Procedural aspects may also be relevant: initiator of the prosecution (whistle-blower, nongovernmental organization, FIU, anticorruption agency) and related offenses.

Requested states may seek explanations regarding the manner in which evidence is collected or legal proceedings are undertaken. This may be necessary to meet the due process requirements of the legal system. Particular attention is likely to be given to evidence collected by coercive means and confessions. It is important to stress that requested authorities should determine whether due process requirements have been met by proceeding on a case-by-case basis rather than by looking at the entire legal system (Kofele-Kale 2006b, n. 145; Schmid 2006, 47). In order to address these concerns, MLA requests will generally have to provide information on domestic proceedings, such as the rights afforded the parties and any procedural decisions taken by the courts regarding the case in question.

Informal cooperation and communication between the requesting and requested jurisdiction can help to clarify the evidentiary requirements and how evidence should be presented before the MLA request is drafted. Communications between parties can also help to identify evidentiary requirements for MLA requests related to specific offenses. Indonesia, for instance, allows for MLA in illicit enrichment cases only when there is evidence that the enrichment arose from criminal activities and that the criminal activity harmed the public or society (ADB and OECD 2007, 161).

Some conditions specified by the requested state may also restrict the way in which the requesting state may use the information provided. Following the principle of specialty, information provided by the requested state should only be used for the purpose requested. This principle seeks to "ensure against a requesting state's breach of trust to a requested state and to avoid prosecutorial abuse against the relator after the requested state obtained *in personam* jurisdiction over the relator." This may present a problem where the requesting state is pursuing an investigation for one offense, such as embezzlement, and decides to drop this charge and proceed with a prosecution for illicit enrichment at a later date. Information provided by the requested state to support the embezzlement charge may not be admissible in illicit enrichment proceedings. Again, a possible solution lies in communication, ensuring that the requested and requesting authorities are aware of the potential uses of the information shared and explore specific restrictions that may apply.

5.3 Legal Cooperation Regime

Bilateral MLA treaties and memoranda of understanding provide a framework for cooperation between jurisdictions, complementing and superseding the requirements under UNCAC. These agreements can be used to clarify how authorities will deal with requests related to specific offenses and thereby reduce uncertainty. For example, Switzerland has long handled the U.S. Securities and Exchange Commission investigations by signing memoranda of understanding that address specific requests. Such agreements can address illicit enrichment if the authorities anticipate that such cases will constitute an important part of their bilateral cooperation.

Familiarity with the procedures and legal requirements of partner countries is probably the most effective way to facilitate mutual legal assistance both in general and in illicit enrichment cases. This familiarity can be gained by contacting partner institutions, undertaking joint training activities, and, most important, initiating requests. The vast majority of countries consulted in the course of this study admitted that they had never filed or received an MLA request in an illicit enrichment case. Familiarity can help to avoid miscommunication over the prosecutorial objectives and legal procedures. It can also help partners to identify strategies for the presentation of evidence.

5.4 Observations

Jurisdictions requesting international cooperation, particularly mutual legal assistance requests, continue to encounter challenges in obtaining assistance from requested states. However, these challenges are often surmountable. Because many states will provide assistance based on the underlying conduct, efforts may be made to ensure that the conduct underlying the offense constitutes an offense in the requested jurisdiction. Therefore, it may be helpful for states to look beyond just the illicit enrichment and to focus on the criminal conduct that generates the wealth prior to making the request. States may also wish to address cooperation regarding illicit enrichment in their bilateral MLA treaties, or memoranda of understanding, if they anticipate that such requests will constitute an important part of their bilateral cooperation.

Appendix A. Illicit Enrichment Provisions

Excerpts from the identified laws may be limited to relevant sections, provisions, and/or articles. In addition, laws appearing in English rather than the original language have been translated for ease and clarity, but are not to be construed as official translations.

Algeria: 2006, Law no. 06-01 on the Prevention and the Fight against Corruption, Article 37, De l'Enrichissement Illicite

> Any public official who cannot reasonably explain the increase of his/her funds in comparison to his/her remuneration shall be sentenced to 2–10 years of imprisonment and a fine of DA 200,000–DA 1,000,000 (dinars) … The illicit offense is considered a continuous offense and results from either acquiring or exploiting illicit assets, whether directly or indirectly.

Angola: 2010, Lei da Probidade Administrativa (Law on Public Probity), Article 25g, Section 7

> Adquirir, para si ou para outrem, no exercício de mandato, cargo, emprego ou função pública, bens de qualquer natureza cujo valor seja desproporcional à evolução do patrimônio ou à renda do agente público.

> Translation: To acquire for oneself or for another, in the exercise of one's duties, responsibilities, employment, or public function, goods of any nature whose value is disproportionate to the capital gains or income of the public servant.

Antigua and Barbuda: 2004, The Prevention of Corruption Act, Article 7, Possession of Unexplained Property and Article 8, Penalty for Offenses

> Article 7. 1. A person who, being or having been a public official, (a) maintains a standard of living above that which is commensurate with his present or past official emoluments or (b) is in control of pecuniary resources or property disproportionate to his present or past official emoluments, unless he gives a satisfactory explanation to the court as to how he was able to maintain such standard of living or how such pecuniary resources or property came under his control, commits an offense.

> 2. Where a court is satisfied in proceedings for an offense under Subsection 1(b) that having regard to the closeness of his relationship with the accused and to other circumstances, there is reason to believe that any person was holding pecuniary resources or property in trust for or otherwise on behalf of the accused or acquired such resources or property the resources or property shall, until the contrary is proved, be presumed to have been in the control of the accused.

Article 8. 1. A person who commits an offense under sections 3, 4, 5, 6, or 7 is liable upon conviction on indictment to a fine not exceeding EC$100,000 (Eastern Caribbean dollars) and to imprisonment for a term not exceeding five years or, in addition to the penalty specified above, the court may do any or all of the following: (i) order the person convicted to pay the public body, and in such manner as the court directs, the amount or value of any property, benefit, or advantage received by him; (ii) forfeit his right to claim any noncontributory gratuity or pension to which he would otherwise have been entitled; (iii) declare any right under any noncontributory pension scheme to which he is entitled to be forfeited; (iv) declare him to be disqualified from holding any public office for a period not exceeding seven years from the date of conviction for the offense.

Argentina: 1964, Argentine Criminal Code, Article 286

Section 2. Será reprimido con reclusión o prisión de dos a seis años, multa del cincuenta por ciento al ciento por ciento del valor del enriquecimiento e inhabilitación absoluta perpetua, el que al ser debidamente requerido, no justificare la procedencia de un enriquecimiento patrimonial apreciable suyo o de persona interpuesta para disimularlo, ocurrido con posterioridad a la asunción de un cargo o empleo público y hasta dos años después de haber cesado en su desempeño.

Section 3. Se entenderá que hubo enriquecimiento no sólo cuando el patrimonio se hubiese incrementado con dinero, cosas o bienes, sino también cuando se hubiesen cancelado deudas o extinguido obligaciones que lo afectaban. La persona interpuesta para disimular el enriquecimiento será reprimida con la misma pena que el autor del hecho.

Translation from OAS (2009c): Section 2. Any person who, when so demanded, fails to justify the origin of any appreciable enrichment for himself or a third party in order to hide it, obtained subsequent to assumption of a public office or employment, and for up to two years after having ceased his duties, shall be punished by imprisonment from two to six years, a fine of 50 percent to 100 percent of the value of the enrichment, and absolute perpetual disqualification. Enrichment will be presumed not only when the person's wealth has been increased with money, things, or goods, but also when his debts have been canceled or his obligations extinguished. The person interposed to dissimulate the enrichment shall be punished by the same penalty as the author of the crime.

Section 3. Any person who, by reason of his position, is required by law to present a sworn statement of assets and maliciously fails to do so shall be punished by imprisonment from 15 days to two years and special perpetual disqualification. The offense is deemed committed when, after due notice of the obligation, the person obligated has not complied with those duties within the time limits established by the applicable law. Any person who maliciously falsifies or omits data required in those sworn statements by the applicable laws and regulations shall be liable to the same penalty.

Bangladesh: 2004, the Anti-corruption Commission Act, Article 27; Prevention of Corruption Act of 1947, Section 5(c), Possession of Property Disproportionate to Known Sources of Income

Anti-corruption Commission Act, Article 27. 1. If there are sufficient and reasonable grounds to believe that a person in his/her own name or any other person on his/her behalf is in possession and has obtained ownership of moveable or immoveable property through dishonest means and the property is not consistent with the known sources of his/her income and if he/she fails to submit to the court during trial a satisfactory explanation for possessing that property, then that person shall be sentenced to a prison term ranging from a minimum of three years to a maximum of 10 years imprisonment, and these properties shall be confiscated.

2. If it is proved during the trial of charges under Subsection (1) that the accused person in his own name or any other person on his/her behalf has obtained ownership or is in possession of moveable or immoveable property not consistent with the known sources of his/her income then the court shall presume that the accused person is guilty of the charges and unless the person rebuts that presumption in court the punishment meted out on the basis of this presumption shall not be unlawful.

Prevention of Corruption Act of 1947, Section 5(c). 1. Any public servant who has in his possession any property, movable or immovable, either in his own name or in the name of any other person, which there is reason to believe to have been acquired by improper means and which is proved to be disproportionate to the known sources of income of such public servant shall, if he fails to account for such possession to the satisfaction of the court trying him, be punishable with imprisonment for a term which may extend to seven years and with a fine, and on such conviction the property found to be disproportionate to the known sources of income of the accused by the court shall be forfeited to the provincial government.

2. The reference in Subsection 1 to property acquired by improper means shall be construed as reference to property acquired by means which are contrary to law or to any rule or instrument having the force of law or by coercion, undue influence, fraud, or misrepresentation within the meaning of the Contract Act, 1872.

Bhutan: 2006, the Anti-Corruption Act of Bhutan, Article 107

Any person who, being or having been a public servant or a person having served or serving under a nongovernmental organization or such other organization using public resources, (a) maintains a standard of living that is not commensurate with his lawful source of income or (b) is in control of pecuniary resources or assets disproportionate to his lawful source of income shall unless he gives a satisfactory explanation to the commission or the court, be guilty of an offense and shall be liable for value-based sentencing in accordance with the Penal Code of Bhutan.

Bolivia: 2010, Ley "Marcelo Quiroga Santa Cruz" de Lucha contra la Corrupción, Article 27, Enriquecimiento Ilícito e Investigación de Fortunas

La servidora pública o servidor público, que no hubiere incrementado desproporcionadamente su patrimonio respecto de sus ingresos legítimos y que no pueda ser justificado, será sancionado con privación de libertad de cinco a 10 años, inhabilitación para el ejercicio de la función pública y/o cargos electos, multa de 200 hasta 500 días y el decomiso de los bienes obtenidos ilegalmente.

Botswana: 1994, Corruption and Economic Crime Act, Article 34, Possession of Unexplained Property

1. The director or any officer of the directorate authorized in writing by the director may investigate any person where there are reasonable grounds to suspect that that person (a) maintains a standard of living above that which is commensurate with his present or past known sources of income or assets or (b) is in control or possession of pecuniary resources or property disproportionate to his present or past known sources of income or assets.

2. A person is guilty of corruption if he fails to give a satisfactory explanation to the director or the officer conducting the investigation under Subsection 1 as to how he was able to maintain such a standard of living or how such pecuniary resources or property came under his control or possession.

3. Where a court is satisfied in any proceedings for an offense under Subsection 2 that, having regard to the closeness of his relationship to the accused and to other relevant circumstances, there is reason to believe that any person was holding pecuniary resources or property in trust for or otherwise on behalf of the accused, or acquired such resources or property as a gift or loan without adequate consideration, from the accused, such resources or property shall, until the contrary is proved, be deemed to have been under the control or in the possession of the accused.

Brunei Darussalam: 1982, Prevention of Corruption Act, Article 12, Possession of Unexplained Property

1. Any person who, being or having been a public officer, (a) maintains a standard of living above that which is commensurate with his present or past emoluments or (b) is in control of pecuniary resources or property disproportionate to his present or past emoluments shall, unless he gives a satisfactory explanation to the court as to how he was able to maintain such a standard of living or how such pecuniary resources or property came under his control, be guilty of an offense: Penalty, a fine of B$30,000 (Brunei dollars) and imprisonment for seven years.

2. In addition to any penalty imposed under Subsection 1 the court may order a person convicted of an offense under Subsection 1 to pay to the government (a) a sum not exceeding the amount of the pecuniary resources or (b) a sum not exceeding the value of the property, the acquisition of which by him was not explained to the satisfaction of the court and any such sum ordered to be paid shall be recoverable as a fine.

3. Where a court is satisfied in proceedings for an offense under Subsection 1 that, having regard to the closeness of his relationship to the accused and to other relevant circumstances, there is reason to believe that any person was holding pecuniary resources or property in trust for or otherwise on behalf of the accused, or acquired such pecuniary resources or property as a gift, or loan without adequate consideration from the accused, such pecuniary resources or property shall, until the contrary is proved, be deemed to have been under the control or in the possession of the accused.

Chile: 1999, Criminal Code of Chile, Article 241

Any public official who while performing his or her position obtains a significant and unjustified increase of his or her equity shall be punished with a fine equal to the improper equity increase and with a penalty of temporary absolute disqualification from holding public office in its minimum or medium degrees.

The stated above shall not be applied if the conduct giving rise to the improper equity increase constitutes, in itself, any of the offenses described in the present title, in which case the penalties assigned to the respective offense will be imposed. The evidence of unjustified enrichment referred in this article shall be always brought by the public prosecution.

If the criminal proceeding starts by informal report or formal complaint and the public officer is acquitted under the offense criminalized in this article or is benefited by a definitive dismissal under Article 250 (a) or (b) of the Criminal Procedural Code, he or she shall be entitled to be indemnified by the person who has filed the informal report or formal complaint of material and moral damages incurred, notwithstanding the criminal liability under Article 211 of this code.

China: 1997, Criminal Law of the People's Republic of China, Article 395

Any state functionary whose property or expenditure obviously exceeds his lawful income, if the difference is enormous, may be ordered to explain the sources of his property. If he cannot prove that the sources are legitimate, the part that exceeds his lawful income shall be regarded as illegal gains, and he shall be sentenced to fixed-term imprisonment of not more than five years or criminal detention, and the part of property that exceeds his lawful income shall be recovered.

Any state functionary shall, in accordance with state regulations, declare to the state his bank savings outside the territory of China. Whoever has a relatively large amount of such savings and does not declare them to the state shall be sentenced to fixed-term imprisonment of not more than two years or criminal detention; if the circumstances are relatively minor, he shall be given administrative sanctions at the discretion of his work unit or the competent authorities at a higher level.

China, Hong Kong SAR: 1971, Prevention of Bribery Ordinance, Section 10

1. Any person who, being or having been the chief executive or a prescribed officer (Amended 14 of 2003, Section 17; 22 of 2008, Section 4), (a) maintains a standard of living above that which is commensurate with his present or past official emoluments or (b) is in control of pecuniary resources or property disproportionate to his present or past official emoluments shall, unless he gives satisfactory explanation to the court as to how he was able to maintain such a standard of living or how such pecuniary resources or property came under his control, be guilty of an offense.

2. Any person guilty of an offense under this part, other than an offense under Section 3, shall be liable (a) on conviction on indictment (i) for an offense under Section 10, to a fine of HK$1,000,000 (Hong Kong dollars) and to imprisonment for 10 years; (ii) for an offense under Section 5 or 6, to a fine of HK$500,000 and to imprisonment for 10 years, and (iii) for any other offense under this part, to a fine of HK$500,000 and to imprisonment for seven years; and (replaced 50 of 1987, Section 3) (b) on summary conviction (i) for an offense under

section 10, to a fine of HK$500,000 and to imprisonment for three years; and (ii) for any other offense under this part, to a fine of HK$100,000 and to imprisonment for three years, and shall be ordered to pay to such person or public body and in such manner as the court directs, the amount or value of any advantage received by him or such part thereof as the court may specify.

3. In addition to any penalty imposed under Subsection 1, the court may order a person convicted of an offense under Section 10(1)(b) to pay to the government (Amended 1 of 2003, Section 3) (a) a sum not exceeding the amount of the pecuniary resources or (b) a sum not exceeding the value of the property, the acquisition of which by him was not explained to the satisfaction of the court.

China, Macao SAR: 2003, Law 11/2003, Statement of Incomes and Properties

1. The statement required pursuant to Article 1. Which shall by himself or through intermediaries are in possession of assets or income abnormally higher than indicated in previous statements and provided no warrant, specifically, how and when they came into his possession or not satisfactorily demonstrate their lawful origin shall be punished with imprisonment up to three years and a fine of up to 360 days' pay.

2. The illicit assets or income identified under the preceding paragraph may, following a court conviction, be declared forfeit in favor of the Macao Special Administrative Region.

Colombia: 2004, Código Penal, Artículo 412, Enriquecimiento Ilícito (penalties increased by Article 14 of Law 890 of 2004, as of January 1, 2005)

El servidor público que durante su vinculación con la administración, o quien haya desempeñado funciones públicas y en los dos años siguientes a su desvinculación, obtenga, para sí o para otro, incremento patrimonial injustificado, siempre que la conducta no constituya otro delito, incurrirá en prisión de 96 a 180 meses, multa equivalente al doble del valor del enriquecimiento sin que supere el equivalente a 50,000 salarios mínimos legales mensuales vigentes, e inhabilitación para el ejercicio de derechos y funciones públicas de 96 a 180 meses.

Translation from OAS (2010c): Any public servant who, while in government employment, or anyone who has performed public duties and who, in that time or in a period of two years thereafter, obtains for themselves or for another an unjustified increase in wealth shall, provided that the conduct does not constitute another offense, be liable to between 96 and 180 months of imprisonment, a fine of twice the amount of the enrichment without that exceeding 50,000 times the statutory monthly minimum wage in force, and ineligibility from the exercise of rights and public duties for between 96 and 180 months.

Costa Rica: 2004, Law 8422: Law against Corruption and Illicit Enrichment in Public Office, Article 45

Será sancionado con prisión de tres a seis años quien, aprovechando ilegítimamente el ejercicio de la función pública o la custodia, la explotación, el uso o la administración de fondos, servicios, o bienes públicos, bajo cualquier título o modalidad de gestión, por sí o por interpósita persona física o jurídica, acreciente su patrimonio, adquiera bienes, goce derechos, cancele deudas o extinga obligaciones que afecten su patrimonio o el de personas jurídicas, en cuyo capital social tenga participación ya sea directamente o por medio de otras personas jurídicas.

Cuba: 1987, Código Penal, Ley no. 62, Chapter 3, Article 150, Ejercicio Fraudulento de Funciones Públicas, Section 3, Enriquecimiento Ilícito

1. La autoridad, funcionario, o empleado que, directamente o por persona intermedia, realiza gastos o aumenta su patrimonio o el de un tercero en cuantía no proporcional a sus ingresos legales, sin justificar la licitud de los medios empleados para realizar los gastos u obtener tal aumento patrimonial, incurre en sanción de privación de libertad de dos a cinco años o multa de 300 a 1,000 cuotas o ambas.

2. A los declarados responsables del delito previsto en este artículo se les impone, además, la sanción accesoria de confiscación de bienes.

3. Las sanciones previstas en este artículo se imponen siempre que el hecho no constituya un delito de mayor entidad.

Ecuador: 1971, Penal Code of Ecuador, Article 296.1, Del Enriquecimiento Ilícito

1. Constituye enriquecimiento ilícito el incremento injustificado del patrimonio de una persona, producido con ocasión o como consecuencia del desempeño de un cargo o función pública, que no sea el resultado de sus ingresos legalmente percibidos.

2. El enriquecimiento ilícito se sancionará con la pena de dos a cinco años de prisión y la restitución del duplo del monto del enriquecimiento ilícito, siempre que no constituya otro delito.

Translation from OAS (2010d): 1. Illicit enrichment is the unexplained increase in the wealth of a person produced in the course of, or as a consequence of, the performance of a public duty or function that is not the result of legally received income.

2. Illicit enrichment shall be punished with a sentence of two to five years of imprisonment and the repayment of twice the amount of the illicit enrichment, provided that it does not constitute another offense.

Egypt, Arab Rep. : Law no. 62 of 1975, Illegitimate Gains

1. Those responsible for public authority and all employees in the state administrative body except for those of the third level.

2. All money gained by any of those subjected to the rules of this law for him or for others as a result of exploiting the service or qualification or as a result of a behavior contrary to the penal law or public behavior is considered illegitimate gain.

It is considered to be the result of the exploitation of the service or qualification or the illegal conduct an increase in wealth that occurs after assuming the service or establishing the qualification for those who are subjected to the law, his spouse or minor children whenever it is not proportionate with their income and in the case of failing to prove legitimate source for it.

18. A person who has collected for himself or for others illegitimate gains shall be punished by imprisonment and a fine equivalent to the illegitimate gain in addition to a rule to return that gain.

The criminal case which ends by death does not prevent the return of the illegitimate gains according to a ruling from the relevant criminal court at the request of one of the authorities stipulated in Article 5 within three years of the date of the death.

The court has to order the spouse and minor children who have benefited from the illegitimate gain to execute the ruling to return the money each according to the extent of his or her benefit. The court may also order those who have seriously benefited other than those mentioned in the previous paragraph to be included, so that the judgment to return would be enforceable and taken from his or her money in the same amount of the benefits acquired.

El Salvador: Constitution, Article 240; Criminal Code, Article 333 (Illicit Enrichment)

Constitution, Article 240. Those public officials and employees that unlawfully enrich themselves at the expense of the government or municipal treasury shall be required to make restitution to the state or municipality for what they improperly acquired without prejudice to their liability under the law.

Illicit enrichment is presumed when the increase in the capital of the public official or employee, counted from the date on which they took up their position until the date of their termination, is significantly higher than it normally would be based on their lawful pay and emoluments and the increases in their capital or income by any other lawful cause. In determining that increase, the capital and income of the public official or employee, their spouse, and their children shall be jointly considered.

Those public officials and employees that the law determines are required to declare their wealth to the Supreme Court of Justice in accordance with the preceding clauses within 60 days after taking up their duties. The court has the authority to take the measures it deems necessary to verify the accuracy of the declaration, which it shall keep confidential and which shall serve exclusively for the purpose provided in this article. The aforementioned public officials and employees shall submit a new declaration of their wealth upon termination of their duties. The law shall determine the penalties for breach of this obligation.

Judicial proceedings for unlawful enrichment may only be instituted within 10 years after the date on which the public official or employee ceased to hold the office in whose exercise said enrichment may have occurred.

Criminal Code, Article 333. Any government official, public authority, or public employee who in the course of their duties or functions obtains an unjustified increase in wealth shall be punished with three to 10 years of imprisonment.

Third parties who disguise an unjustified increase in wealth shall be liable to the same penalty.

Whatever the case, they shall be disqualified from that position or employment for the same period of time.

Ethiopia: 2004, the Criminal Code of the Federal Democratic Republic of Ethiopia Proclamation no. 414/2004

1. Any public servant, being or having been in a public office, who (a) maintains a standard of living above that which is commensurate with the official income from his present or past employment or other means or (b) is in control of pecuniary resources or property disproportionate to the official income from his present or past employment or other means shall, unless he gives a satisfactory explanation to the court as to how he was able to maintain such a standard of living or how such pecuniary resources or property came under his control, be punished, without prejudice to the confiscation of the property or the restitution to the third party, with simple imprisonment or fine or, in serious cases, with rigorous imprisonment not exceeding five years and a fine.

2. Where the court, during proceeding under Subarticle I(b), is satisfied that there is reason to believe that any person, owing to his closeness to the accused or other circumstances, was holding pecuniary resources or property in trust for or otherwise on behalf of the accused, such resources or property shall, in the absence of evidence to the contrary, be presumed to have been under the control of the accused.

Gabon: 2003, Loi no. 002/2003, Instituant un Régime de Prévention et de Répression de l'Enrichissement Illicite en République Gabonaise

Au sens de la présente loi, est considéré comme enrichissement illicite, le fait, pour tout dépositaire de l'autorité de l'etat, de réaliser ou de tenter de réaliser des profits personnels ou d'obtenir tout autre avantage de tout nature: au moyen d'actes de corruption active ou passive, de concussion, de fraude, de détournement ou de soustraction frauduleuse de deniers ou de biens publics, d'abus de pouvoir, de trafic d'influence, de prise illégale d'intérêts ou de tout autre procédé illicite; au moyen d'une pratique illicite en matière d'expropriation, d'obtention de marché, de concession ou de permis d'exportation ou d'importation; par l'utilisation indue, á son profit ou á celui d'un tiers, de tout type d'information confidentielle ou privilégiée dont il a eu connaissance en raison ou á l'occasion de ses fonctions. Est également considéré comme enrichissement illicite, l'augmentation significative du patrimoine de tout dépositaire de l'autorité de l'etat que celui-ci ne peut raisonnablement justifier par rapport aux revenus qu'il a légitimement perçus.

Article 24. Tout fonctionnaire, tout agent ou préposé d'une administration publique, chargé, à raison même de sa fonction, de la surveillance ou du contrôle direct d'une entreprise privée et qui, soit en position de congé ou de disponibilité, soit après admission à la retraite, soit après démission, destitution ou révocation, et pendant un délai de cinq ans à compter de la cessation de la fonction, prendra ou recevra une participation par travail, conseils ou capitaux, sauf par dévolution héréditaire en ce qui concerne les capitaux dans la concession, entreprise ou régie qui était directement soumise à sa surveillance ou à son contrôle, et ce en connaissance de cause, sera puni des peines prévues à l'article 21 ci-dessus.

Les dirigeants des concessions, entreprises, ou régies publiques sont considérés comme complices effectués ou des biens livrés.

Article 21. Tout dépositaire de l'autorité de l'etat qui, soit ouvertement, soit par actes simulés, soit par personnes interposées, aura, en connaissance de cause, dans les actes, adjudications ou régies dont il a eu l'administration ou la surveillance, dans les entreprises privées, les établissements publics ou parapublics soumis à sa surveillance ou à son contrôle, dans les marchés ou contrats passés au nom de l'etat avec l'une des entreprises visées ci-dessus, pris ou reçu quelque intérêt que ce soit, sera puni d'un emprisonnement de deux ans au moins et de dix ans au plus et à une amende de CFAF 2,000,000 à 20,000,000 (CFA francs).

Il sera, à jamais, déclaré incapable d'exercer un emploi ou une charge publique.

La présente disposition s'applique également à tout dépositaire de l'autorité de l'etat qui aura, en connaissance de cause, pris un intérêt quelconque dans une affaire dont il était directement chargé d'ordonnancer le paiement ou de faire la liquidation.

Guyana: 1998, Integrity Commission Act

1. Where a person who is or was a person in public life, or any other person on his behalf, is found to be in possession of property or pecuniary resource disproportionate to the known sources of income of the first mentioned person, and that person fails to produce satisfactory evidence to prove that the possession of the property or pecuniary resource was acquired by lawful means, he shall be guilty of an offense and shall be liable, on summary conviction, to a fine and to imprisonment for a term of not less than six months nor more than three years.

2. In imposing a fine under Subsection 1 on a person found guilty of an offense under that subsection, the court shall have regard to the value of the property or pecuniary resource in the possession of that person, which cannot be accounted for by his known sources of income or other lawful means of acquisition of the property or pecuniary resource and such fine shall be equivalent to one and one half times the value of the aforesaid property or pecuniary resource found to be in the possession of said person.

Honduras: 1993, Ley Contra el Enrequicimiento Ilícito de los Servidores Público Decreto no. 301

Se presume enriquecimiento ilícito cuando el aumento del capital del funcionario o empleado, desde la fecha en que haya tomado posesión de su cargo hasta aquella en que haya cesado en sus funciones, fuere notablemente superior al que normalmente hubiere podido tener en virtud de los sueldos y emolumentos que haya percibido legalmente y de los incrementos de su capital o de sus ingresos por cualquier otra causa.

Para determinar dicho aumento, el capital y los ingresos del servidor público, con los de sus cónyuge, compañero o compañera de hogar, hijos sujetos a patria potestad y pupilos se considerarán en conjunto.

Para justificar la presunción de enriquecimiento ilícito del servidor público, se tomará en cuenta: sus condiciones económicas personales previas al ejercicio del cargo o empleo; la cuantía en que ha aumentado su capital en relación al monto de sus ingresos y de sus gastos ordinarios; y la ejecución de otros actos o la existencia de otras circunstancias que permitan presumir que la persona ha incurrido en alguno de los casos de enriquecimiento ilícito a que se refiere el Artículo 7 de esta ley.

Article 9. La carga de la prueba sobre las circunstancias indicadas en los artículos anteriores, la relativa al importe de ingresos y de gastos ordinarios y la que tienda a comprobar la licitud del aumento de capital, pesa sobre el servidor público.

Article 32. El delito de enriquecimiento ilícito será castigado, según el monto del enriquecimiento, así: (a) si dicho enriquecimiento no excediere de L 5,000 (lempiras), con presidio menor en su grado máximo; (b) si dicho enriquecimiento excediere de L 5,000 y no pasare de L 10,000, con presidio mayor en su grado mínimo; (c) si excediere de L 10,000 y no pasare de L 100,000, con presidio mayor en su grado medio; y (d) si excediere de L 100,000, con presidio mayor en su grado máximo.

India: 1988, Prevention of Corruption Act, Article 13, Criminal Misconduct by a Public Servant

1. A public servant is said to commit the offense of criminal misconduct, (a) ... (e) if he or any person on his behalf, is in possession or has, at any time during the period of his office, been in possession for which the public servant cannot satisfactorily account, of pecuniary resources or property disproportionate to his known sources of income.

This offense is also punishable with a minimum imprisonment of one year, extendable up to seven years, and also with a fine.

Jamaica: 2005, Corruption (Prevention) Act

Section 14.1. A public servant commits an act of corruption if he (a) owns assets disproportionate to his lawful earnings and (b) upon being requested by the commission or any person duly authorized to investigate an allegation of corruption against him, to provide an explanation as to how he came by such assets, he (i) fails to do so or (ii) gives an explanation which is not considered to be satisfactory, he shall be liable to prosecution for the offense of illicit enrichment and, on conviction thereof, to the penalties specified in Section 15(1).

Section 5(A). It shall be a defense to a person charged with an offense of illicit enrichment to show the court that he came by the assets by lawful means.

Section 15. 1. Any person who commits an act of corruption commits an offense as is liable (a) on summary conviction in a resident magistrate's court, (i) in the case of a first offense, to a fine not exceeding J$1 million (Jamaica dollars) or to imprisonment for a term not exceeding two years, or to both such fine and imprisonment and (ii) in the case of a second or subsequent offense, to a fine not exceeding J$3 million or to imprisonment for a term not exceeding three years or to both such fine and imprisonment.

2. On conviction in a circuit court, (i) in the case of a first offense to a fine not exceeding J$5 million or to imprisonment for a term not exceeding five years or to both such fine and imprisonment and (ii) in the case of a second or subsequent offense, to a fine not exceeding J$10 million or to imprisonment for a term not exceeding 10 years or to both such fine and imprisonment.

Lebanon: 1999, Illicit Wealth Law no. 154

Article 1. Illicit wealth is considered as (1) wealth earned by the employee or person performing public service and the judge or their accomplice, by bribery or influence peddling or misuse of position, or work assigned to them (Articles 351 to 366 of the Penal Code), or by any illegal means even if it does not constitute a criminal offense; (2) enrichment of an employee or person performing public service, the judge and other natural or legal persons, either through acquisition or through the attainment of export and import licenses or other benefits of different types, if done contrary to the law; (3) obtainment or poor implementation of contracts, concessions, and licenses granted by any person of public law to bring in benefit, if done contrary to the law.

Article 9. The provisions of the criminal procedures law apply to the investigation in illicit wealth cases, and the provisions of the criminal code apply in cases of illicit wealth as a result of a criminal offense.

Lesotho: 1999, Prevention of Corruption and Economic Offenses Act no. 5

Possession of unexplained property. Section 31(1). The director or any officer of the directorate authorized in writing by the director may investigate any public officer where there are reasonable grounds to suspect that person (a) maintains a standard of living above that which is commensurate with his present or past known source of income or assets reasonably suspected to have been acquired illegally or (b) is in control or possession of pecuniary resources or property disproportionate to his present or past known sources of income or assets reasonably suspected to have been acquired illegally.

2. A public officer is presumed to have committed the offense of corruption if he fails to give a satisfactory explanation to the director or the officer conducting the investigation under Subsection 1 as to how he was able to maintain such a standard of living or how such pecuniary resources or property came under his control or possession.

3. Where a court is satisfied in any proceedings for an offense under Subsection 2 that, having regard to the closeness of his relationship to the accused and to other relevant circumstances, there is reason to believe that any person was holding pecuniary resources or property as a gift, or loan without adequate consideration from the accused, such resources or property shall, until the contrary is proved, be deemed to have been under the control or in the possession of the accused.

4. Any person who commits the offense of corruption or cheating the revenue under this part shall, upon conviction, be liable to a fine not less than M 5,000.00 (maloti) and not more than M 10,000.00 or to imprisonment for a term not less than five years and not more than 10 years or both and in the case of juristic persons, the fine shall not be less than M 10,000.00.

Macedonia, FYR: 1996, Criminal Code, Illicit Enrichment and Concealment of Property, Article 359(a)

1. An official person or responsible person in public enterprise, public institution, or other legal entity who disposes of state capital, and contrary to the legal obligation to report property status or its change provides false or incomplete information for his/her property

or for the property of his/her family members, which significantly exceeds his/her legal income, shall be sentenced to imprisonment of six months to five years and with a fine.

2. The sentence referred to in paragraph 1 of this article shall be applied for an official person or responsible person in public enterprise, public institution, or other legal entity that disposes of state capital, when it is established in legally determined procedure that in the course of holding a position or performing duty he/she or a member of his/her family has obtained property which significantly exceeds his/her legal incomes, has provided false data, or conceals the real sources of the property.

3. If the crime referred to in paragraphs 1 and 2 of this article is committed in terms of property that largely exceeds the perpetrator's legal incomes, she/he shall be sentenced to imprisonment of one to eight years and with a fine.

4. The perpetrator shall not be punished for the actions referred to in paragraphs 2 and 3 of this article, if he/she provides acceptable explanation about the origin of the property during the procedure before the court.

5. The property exceeding the incomes that the perpetrator legally obtains and for which the perpetrator has provided false or incomplete data or has not provided data or has concealed its real sources shall be confiscated, and if the confiscation is not possible, then other property of the perpetrator of equivalent value shall be confiscated.

6. The property referred to in paragraph 5 of this article shall be confiscated from the members of perpetrator's family for which the property has been obtained or to whom it has been transferred if it is evident that they have not provided compensation equivalent to its value, as well as from third persons if they do not prove that they have provided compensation equivalent to its value.

Madagascar: 2004, Law no. 2004-030 on the Fight against Corruption

Will be punished with an imprisonment of six months to five years and a fine of FMG 50 million (Malagasy francs) or MGA 10 million (ariary) to FMG 200 million or MGA 40 million, any person invested with public authority or in charge of a public service mission, any person invested with a public electoral mandate, any leader, proxy, or employee of a public company that cannot reasonably justify a substantial increase in such person's personal wealth relative to his or her lawful revenues will be punished with the same penalties as any person that will have knowingly held the goods or resources of the persons cited above.

Illicit enrichment is a continuous offense characterized by the holding of personal wealth and the use of illicit resources. Evidence of the licit origin of the enrichment or the resources can be brought forth by any means. However, will be exempted from prosecution pursuant to this article the person who, before the opening of an inquiry or direct citation, will have revealed facts to the administrative or legal authorities and permitted the identification and condemnation of the principal author.

The decision of condemnation may also pronounce the confiscation for the benefit of the state, government organization, public, and para-public organisms, of all or part of the condemned party's assets up to the amount of the prejudice sustained.

Malawi: 1995, Corrupt Practices Act

Section 32. 1. The director, the deputy director, or any officer of the bureau authorized in writing by the director may investigate any public officer where there are reasonable grounds to believe that such public officer (a) maintains a standard of living above that which is commensurate with his present or past official emoluments or other known sources of income; (b) is in control or possession of pecuniary resources or property disproportionate to his present or past official emoluments or other known sources of income; or (c) is directly or indirectly in receipt of the benefit of any services which he may reasonably be suspected of having received corruptly or in circumstances which amount to an offense under this act.

2. Any public officer who, after due investigation carried out under the provisions of Subsection 1, is found to (a) maintain a standard of living above that which is commensurate with his present or past official emoluments or other known sources of income; (b) be in control or possession of pecuniary resources or property disproportionate to his present or past official emoluments or other known sources of income; or (c) be in receipt directly or indirectly of the benefit of any services which he may reasonably be suspected of having received corruptly or in circumstances which amount to an offense under this act, shall, unless he gives a reasonable explanation, be charged with having or having had under his control or in his possession pecuniary resources or property reasonably suspected of having been corruptly acquired and, unless he gives a satisfactory explanation to the court as to how else he was able to maintain such a standard of living, or such pecuniary resources or property came under his control or his possession, or he came to enjoy the benefits of such services, he shall be guilty of an offense.

3. In this section, (i) "official emoluments" includes a pension, gratuity, or other terminal benefits; (ii) "public officer" includes any person who has held office as a public officer on or after 6th July 1964.

Section 34. Any person who is guilty of an offense under this part shall be liable to imprisonment for a term of 12 years.

Section 35. Any person who attempts to commit, or who aids, abets, counsels, or conspires with any person to commit, an offense under this part shall be guilty of committing that offense.

Malaysia: 1997, Anti-Corruption Act, Article 32

Where the public prosecutor has reasonable grounds to believe that any officer of a public body who has been served with the written notice referred to in Subsection 1 owns, possesses, controls, or holds any interest in any property which is excessive, having regard to his present or past emoluments and all other relevant circumstances, the public prosecutor may by written direction require him to furnish a statement on oath or affirmation explaining how he was able to own, possess, control, or hold such excess and if he fails to explain satisfactorily such excess, he shall be guilty of an offense and shall on conviction be liable to (a) imprisonment for a term of not less than 14 days and not more than 20 years and (b) a fine which is not less than five times the value of the excess, if the excess is capable of being valued, or RM 20,000 (ringgit), whichever is the higher.

Mexico: 2003, Federal Penal Code, Article 224, Enriquecimiento Ilícito

Se sancionará a quien con motivo de su empleo, cargo, o comisión en el servicio público, haya incurrido en enriquecimiento ilícito. Existe enriquecimiento ilícito cuando el servidor público no pudiere acreditar el legítimo aumento de su patrimonio o la legítima procedencia de los bienes a su nombre o de aquellos respecto de los cuales se conduzca como dueño, en los términos de la Ley Federal de Responsabilidades de los Servidores Públicos.

Incurre en responsabilidad penal, asimismo, quien haga figurar como suyos bienes que el servidor público adquiera o haya adquirido en contravención de lo dispuesto en la misma ley, a sabiendas de esta circunstancia. Al que cometa el delito de enriquecimiento ilícito se le impondrán las siguientes sanciones:

Decomiso en beneficio del estado de aquellos bienes cuya procedencia no se logre acreditar de acuerdo con la Ley Federal de Responsabilidades de los Servidores Públicos.

Cuando el monto a que ascienda el enriquecimiento ilícito no exceda del equivalente de 5,000 veces el salario mínimo diario vigente en el Distrito Federal, se impondrán de tres meses a dos años de prisión, multa de 30 a 300 veces el salario mínimo diario vigente en el Distrito Federal al momento de cometerse el delito y destitución e inhabilitación de tres meses a dos años para desempeñar otro empleo, cargo, o comisión públicos.

Cuando el monto a que ascienda el enriquecimiento ilícito exceda del equivalente de 5,000 veces el salario mínimo diario vigente en el Distrito Federal, se impondrán de dos años a 14 años de prisión, multa de 300 a 500 veces el salario mínimo diario vigente en el Distrito Federal al momento de cometerse el delito y destitución e inhabilitación de dos años a 14 años para desempeñar otro empleo, cargo o comisión públicos.

Translation from OAS (2010e): Sanctions shall apply to anyone who commits illicit enrichment by reason of his post, position, or commission. Illicit enrichment exists when a public servant is unable to prove the legitimacy of an increase in his net worth or the legal origin of assets held in his name or with respect to which he acts as the owner, pursuant to the Federal Law on the Responsibilities of Public Servants.

Criminal responsibility is also incurred by a person who knowingly passes off, as his own, assets acquired by a public servant in contravention of the provisions of this law.

The following sanctions shall apply to those who commit the crime of illicit enrichment: Forfeiture, to the benefit of the state, of those assets that cannot be accredited in accordance with the Federal Law on the Responsibilities of Public Servants.

When the amount of the illicit enrichment does not exceed the equivalent of 5,000 times the minimum daily wage in force in the Federal District, the sanction shall be a prison term of between three months and two years, a fine of between 30 and 300 times the minimum daily wage in force in the Federal District at the time the crime was committed, dismissal and disqualification from holding another public post, position, or commission for between three months and two years.

When the amount of the illicit enrichment exceeds the equivalent of 5,000 times the minimum daily wage in force in the Federal District, the sanction shall be a prison term of between two and 14 years, a fine of between 300 and 500 times the minimum daily wage in force in the Federal District at the time the crime was committed, dismissal and disqualification from holding another public post, position, or commission for between two and 14 years.

Nepal: 2009, the Prevention of Corruption Act, Article 20, Property Deemed to Be Acquired Illegally

1. In case the statement of property submitted in accordance with prevailing laws by a public servant deemed to have held a public office in accordance with prevailing laws seems to be incompatible or unnatural or in case he maintains an incompatible or unsuitable lifestyle or it is proved that he has given someone a donation, gift, grant, present or has lent money beyond his capacity, he shall prove the sources from which he has acquired such property, and if he fails to do so, such property shall be deemed to have been acquired in an illegal manner.

2. In case it has been proved that a public servant has acquired property in an illegal manner as referred to in Subsection 1, he shall be liable to a punishment of imprisonment for a term not exceeding two years as per the amount of the property acquired in such a manner and a fine according to the amount of property, and the illegal property acquired in such a manner shall also be confiscated.

Nicaragua: 2008, Law no. 641 of 2008 (Criminal Code), Article 448, Enriquecimiento Ilícito

La autoridad, funcionario, o empleado público, que sin incurrir en un delito más severamente penado, obtenga un incremento de su patrimonio con significativo exceso, respecto de sus ingresos legítimos, durante el ejercicio de sus funciones y que no pueda justificar razonablemente su procedencia, al ser requerido por el órgano competente señalado en la ley, será sancionado de tres a seis años de prisión e inhabilitación por el mismo período para ejercer cargos o empleos públicos.

Translation from OAS (2010f): A public authority, official, or employee who, without committing a more severely punished crime, obtains an increase in his net worth that is significantly excessive compared to his legitimate income during the performance of his functions and the origin of which he cannot reasonably justify, when so required to do by the competent body indicated by law, shall be punished by a prison term of between three and six years and disqualified from holding public positions or posts for the same duration.

Niger: 1992, Ordonnance no. 92-024 du 18 Juin 1992, Portant Répression de l'Enrichissement Illicite

Article 1. Le délit d'enrichissement illicite est constitué lorsqu'il est établi qu'une personne possède un patrimoine et/ou mène un train de vie que ses revenus licites ne lui permettent pas de justifier.

Article 4. Dès lors qu'est ouverte une information pour enrichissement illicite, le ministère public adresse une réquisition à la personne visée par ladite information afin qu'elle lui communique l'état de son patrimoine et les modalités de sa constitution; la nature et le montant de ses revenus.

Pakistan: 1999, National Accountability Ordinance, Article 9, Corruption and Corrupt Practices; Prevention of Corruption Act 1947 (amended in 1960), Section 5-C, Possession of Property Disproportionate to Known Sources of Income

National Accountability Ordinance, Article 9. A holder of a public office, or any other person, is said to commit or to have committed the offense of corruption and corrupt practices: ... (v) If he or any of his dependents or *benamidars* owns, possesses, or has any right or title in any movable or immovable property or pecuniary resources disproportionate to his known sources of income, which he cannot reasonably account for.

All offenses under this order shall be non-bailable and, notwithstanding anything contained in Sections 426, 491, 497, 498, and 561A or any other provision of the code, or any other law for the time being in force, no court including the High Court shall have jurisdiction to grant bail to any person accused of any offense under this order.

Prevention of Corruption Act 1947, Section 5-C. 1. Any public servant who has in his possession any property, moveable or immoveable either in his own name or in the name of any other person, which there is reason to believe to have been acquired by improper means and which is proved to be disproportionate to the known sources of income of such public servant shall, if he fails to account for such possession to the satisfaction of the court trying him, be punishable with imprisonment for a term which may extend to seven years and with a fine, and on such conviction the property found to be disproportionate to the known sources of income of the accused by the court shall be forfeited to the provincial government.

The reference in Subsection 1 to property acquired by improper means shall be construed as a reference to property acquired by means which are contrary to law or to any rule or instrument having the force of law or by coercion, undue influence, fraud, or misrepresentation within the meaning of the Contract Act, 1872.

Panama: 2008, Penal Code of Panama, Article 345, Enriquecimiento Injustificado

El servidor público que, personalmente o por interpuesta persona, incremente indebidamente su patrimonio respecto a los ingresos legítimos obtenidos durante el ejercicio de su cargo y hasta cinco años después de haber cesado en el cargo, y cuya procedencia lícita no pueda justificar será sancionado con prisión de tres a seis años.

La pena será de seis a doce años de prisión si lo injustificadamente obtenido supera la suma de B 100,000 (balboas).

La misma sanción se aplicará a la persona interpuesta para disimular el incremento patrimonial no justificado.

Para efectos de esta disposición, se entenderá que hay enriquecimiento injustificado, no solo cuando el patrimonio se hubiera aumentado con dinero, cosas, o bienes, respecto a sus ingresos legítimos, sino también cuando se hubieran cancelado deudas o extinguido obligaciones que lo afectaban.

Translation from OAS (2010g): Any public servant who, either personally or through a third party, unduly increases their wealth in relation to the legitimate income obtained during the occupation of their post and for up to five years after having left the post, whose lawful provenance they are unable to show, shall be punished with three to six years of imprisonment.

The penalty shall be six to 12 years of imprisonment if the unjustified amount obtained exceeds the sum of B 100,000.00 (balboas).

The same penalty shall apply to the third party used to conceal the unjustified increase in wealth.

For the purposes of this provision, unjustified enrichment shall be deemed to exist not only when there has been an increase in wealth in terms of money, objects, or property in relation to their lawful income, but also when debts have been repaid or obligations extinguished.

Paraguay: 2004, Ley no. 2.523/04, Article 3, Que Previene, Tipifica, y Sanciona el Enriquecimiento Ilícito en la Función Pública y el Tráfico de Influencias

1. Comete hecho punible de enriquecimiento ilícito y será sancionado con pena privativa de libertad de uno a 10 años, el funcionario público comprendido en cualquiera de las situaciones previstas en el Artículo 2º, quien con posterioridad al inicio de su función, incurra en cualquiera de las siguientes situaciones: (a) haya obtenido la propiedad, la posesión, o el usufructo de bienes, derechos, o servicios, cuyo valor de adquisición, posesión o usufructo sobrepase sus legítimas posibilidades económicas, y los de su cónyuge o conviviente; (b) haya cancelado, luego de su ingreso a la función pública, deudas o extinguido obligaciones que afectaban su patrimonio, el de su cónyuge o su conviviente, y sus parientes hasta el segundo grado de consanguinidad y de afinidad, en condiciones que sobrepasen sus legítimas posibilidades económicas.

2. Será aplicable también a los casos previstos en el inciso 1 de este artículo, la pena complementaria prevista en el Artículo 57 del Código Penal.

Translation from OAS (2009d): Article 3 provides that the offense of illicit enrichment is committed by any public servant covered by any of the situations described in Article 234 who, following commencement of his or her functions, incurs any of the following situations: (a) has obtained the ownership, possession, or use and enjoyment of goods, rights, or services that represent a price for purchase, possession, or use and enjoyment that is in excess of his or her legitimate economic possibilities and those of his or her spouse or companion; (b) following his or her admission to public service, has paid off debts or canceled obligations that affected his or her net worth, or those of his/her spouse or companion or relatives up to the second degree by blood and or marriage, in conditions in excess of his/her legitimate economic possibilities.

Peru: 1991, Law 28355 of 2004, Enriquecimiento Illicito (law amending various articles in the Criminal Code and the Law against Money Laundering), which modifies Article 401 (on illicit enrichment) of the Peruvian Criminal Code

El funcionario o servidor público que ilícitamente incrementa su patrimonio, respect de sus ingresos legítomos durante el ejercicio de sus funciones y que no pueda justificar razonablemente, será reprimido con pena privative de libertad no menor de cinco ni mayor de 10 años e inhabilitación conforme a los incisos 1 y 2 del Articulo 36° del Código Penal.

Si el agente es un funcionario público que haya ocupado do cargos de alta dirección en las entidades u organismos de la administración pública o empresas estatales, o esté sometido a la prerrogativa del antejuicio y la acusación constitucional, la pena será no menor de ocho ni mayor de 18 años e inhabilitación conforme a los incisos 1 y 2 del Artículo 36° del Código Penal.

Se considera que existe indicio de enriquecimiento ilícito cuando el aumento del patrimonio y/o del gasto económico personal del funcionario o servidor público, en consideración a su declaración jurada de bienes y rentas, es notoriamente superior al que normalmente haya podido tener en virtud de sus sueldos o emolumentos percibidos, o de los incrementos de su capital, o de sus ingresos por cualquier otra causa lícita.

Translation: Any government official or public servant who unlawfully increases their assets above their lawful earnings during the performance of their functions and cannot reasonably justify said increase, shall be punished with not less than five nor more than 10 years of imprisonment and ineligibility pursuant to Article 36(1) and (2) of the Criminal Code.

If the agent is a government official who has held senior management positions in entities or agencies of the public administration or state-owned enterprises, or is subject to impeachment proceedings, the penalty shall be not less than eight, nor more than 18, years of imprisonment and ineligibility pursuant to Article 36(1) and (2) of the Criminal Code.

Indicia of illicit enrichment are deemed to exist when the increase in the assets and/or personal spending of the government official or public servant, bearing in mind their sworn declaration of assets and income, is clearly higher than it normally could have been based on their pay or emoluments received or on any increases in their equity or income for any other lawful reason.

Philippines: 1978, Anti-Graft and Corrupt Practices Act, Section 8, Prima facie Evidence of and Dismissal due to Unexplained Wealth

If in accordance with the provisions of Republic Act no. 1379, a public official has been found to have acquired during his incumbency, whether in his name or in the name of other persons, an amount of property and/or money manifestly out of proportion to his salary and to his other lawful income, that fact shall be grounds for dismissal or removal. Properties in the name of the spouse and unmarried children of such public official may be taken into consideration, when their acquisition through legitimate means cannot be satisfactorily shown. Bank deposits shall be taken into consideration in the enforcement of this section, notwithstanding any provision of law to the contrary.

Rwanda: 2003, Article 24 de la Loi no. 23/2003, Relative à la Prévention et à la Répression de la Corruption et des Infractions Connexes

Article 24. Se sera rendu coupable d'enrichissement illicite, tout agent de l'etat et toute autre personne qui se sera enrichi sans pouvoir prouver que cet enrichissement est juste et légal. Sera puni d'une peine d'emprisonnement de deux à cinq ans et d'une amende portée au double jusqu'à 10 fois la valeur du bien dont il n'est pas à mesure de justifier l'origine licite.

La juridiction ordonne d'office la confiscation des biens ou des revenus faisant l'objet de l'infraction.

Senegal: 1981, Penal Code of Senegal, Article 163, de l'Enrichissement Illicite

L'enrichissement illicite de tout titulaire d'un mandant public électif ou d'une fonction gouvernementale, de tout magistrat, agent civil ou militaire de l'etat, ou d'une collectivité publique, d'une personne revêtue d'un mandat public, d'un dépositaire public ou d'un officier public ou ministériel, d'un dirigeant ou d'un agent de toute nature des établissements publics, des sociétés nationales, des sociétés d'économie mixte soumises de plein droit au contrôle de l'etat, des personnes morales de droit privé bénéficiant du concours financier de la puissance publique, des ordres professionnels, des organismes privés chargés de l'exécution d'un service public, des associations ou fondations reconnues d'utilité publique, est puni d'un emprisonnement de cinq à 10 ans et d'une amende au moins égale au montant de l'enrichissement et pouvant être portée au double de ce montant.

Le délit d'enrichissement illicite est constitué lorsque, sur simple mise en demeure, une des personnes désignées ci-dessus, se trouve dans l'impossibilité de justifier de l'origine licite des ressources qui lui permettent d'être en possession d'un patrimoine ou de mener un train de vie sans rapport avec ses revenus légaux.

L'origine licite des éléments du patrimoine peut être prouvée par tout moyen. Toutefois la seule preuve d'une libéralité ne suffit pas à justifier de cette origine licite.

Dans le cas où l'enrichissement illicite est réalisé par l'intermédiaire d'un tiers ou d'une personne physique dirigeant la personne morale seront poursuivis comme complices de l'auteur principal.

Sierra Leone: 2008, Anti-Corruption Act, Article 27

1. Any person who, being or having been a public officer having unexplained wealth, (a) maintains a standard of living above that which is commensurate with his present or past official emoluments or (b) is in control of pecuniary resources or property disproportionate to his present or past official emoluments, unless he gives a satisfactory explanation to the court as to how he was able to maintain such a standard of living or how such pecuniary resources or property came under his control, commits an offense.

2. Where the court is satisfied in proceedings for an offense under paragraph b of Subsection 1 that, having regard to the closeness of his relationship to the accused and to other circumstances, there is reason to believe that any person was holding pecuniary resources or property in trust for or otherwise on behalf of the accused or acquired such resources or property as a gift from the accused, such resources or property shall, in the absence of evidence to the contrary, be presumed to have been in the control of the accused.

3. A person guilty of an offense under Subsection 1 shall on conviction be liable to a fine not less than Le 30 million (leones) or to imprisonment for a term not less than three years or to both such fine and imprisonment.

4. In addition to any penalty imposed under Subsection 1, the court may order a person convicted of an offense under paragraph b of Subsection 1 to pay into the Consolidated Fund (a) a sum not exceeding the amount of the pecuniary resources or (b) a sum not exceeding the value of the property, the acquisition by him of which was not explained to the satisfaction of the court.

5. An order under Subsection 4 may be enforced in the same manner as a judgment of the High Court in its civil jurisdiction.

6. In this section, "official emoluments" includes pension or gratuity payable under the National Social Security and Insurance Trust Act no. 5 of 2001.

Uganda: 2009, the Anti-Corruption Act 2009, Section 31, Illicit Enrichment

1. The inspector general of government or the director of public prosecutions or an authorized officer may investigate or cause an investigation of any person where there is reasonable grounds to suspect that the person (a) maintains a standard of living above that which is commensurate with his or her current or past known sources of income or assets or (b) is in control or possession of pecuniary resources or property disproportionate to his or her current or past known sources of income or assets.

2. A person found in possession of illicitly acquired pecuniary resources or property commits an offense and is liable on conviction to a term of imprisonment not exceeding 10 years or a fine not exceeding 240 currency points or both.

3. Where a court is satisfied in any proceedings for an offense under Subsection 2 that having regard to the closeness of his or her relationship to the accused and to the relevant circumstances, there is reason to believe that any person was holding pecuniary resources or property in trust for or otherwise on behalf of the accused, or acquired such resources or property as a gift or loan without adequate consideration from the accused, those resources or property shall, until the contrary is proved, be deemed to have been under the control or in possession of the accused.

4. In any prosecution for corruption or proceedings under this act, a certificate of a government valuer or a valuation expert appointed by the inspector general of government or the director of public prosecutions as the value of the asset or benefit or source of income or benefit is admissible and is proof of the value, unless the contrary is proved.

Venezuela, R.B.: Anti-corruption Law, Article 73

Translation from OAS (2010b): Any public servant who in the performance of his duties obtains an increase in his net worth that is disproportionate in comparison to his income and that he cannot justify, upon being requested so to do and provided that it does not constitute another crime, shall be punished by a prison term of between three and 10 years. The same penalty shall apply to third parties who intervene to cover up such unjustified increases in net worth.

West Bank and Gaza: 2005, Law no.1 of 2005 Concerning Illegal Gains (amended in 2010, now named Anti-Corruption no. 1 of 2005)

Article 1. An illegal gain shall also be any increase in wealth which occurs after the availment of a service or the rendering of a capacity upon a person subject to the provisions of this law or to his spouse or minor descendants, if this is not compatible with their income and the person fails to submit evidence of a legitimate source thereof.

Article 25. Any person who obtains an illegal gain for himself or others, or enables others to do so, shall be punished by the following: (i) temporary imprisonment, (ii) restitution of the value of the illegal gain and of everything that is proven to be in his financial assets and to have been obtained by means of the illegal gains, (iii) payment of a fine that is equal to the value of the illegal gain.

Appendix B. Jurisdictions with Illicit Enrichment Provisions and Rankings for Rule of Law, Control of Corruption, and GDP per Capita, 2009

Jurisdiction	Rule of law (rank out of 214)	Control of corruption (rank out of 211)	GDP per capita (rank out of 174)
Algeria	156	132	85
Angola	187	200	94
Antigua and Barbuda	39	26	49
Argentina	150	131	49
Bangladesh	154	176	148
Bhutan	87	53	128
Bolivia	192	143	110
Botswana	71	52	—
Brunei Darussalam	60	45	—
China	117	135	89
China, Hong Kong SAR	21	13	9
China, Macao SAR	68	68	3
Colombia	129	110	76
Costa Rica	74	58	70
Cuba	147	75	—
Ecuador	197	174	84
Egypt, Arab Rep.	97	125	95
El Salvador	165	99	90
Ethiopia	164	155	163
Gabon	131	173	51
Guyana	143	137	120
Honduras	169	168	114
India	95	113	119
Jamaica	135	127	87

(continued next page)

Jurisdiction	Rule of law (rank out of 214)	Control of corruption (rank out of 211)	GDP per capita (rank out of 174)
Lebanon	145	163	61
Lesotho	113	80	146
Madagascar	158	105	162
Malawi	110	130	168
Malaysia	75	89	55
Mexico	141	108	54
Nepal	175	158	157
Nicaragua	167	160	147
Niger	146	146	170
Pakistan	172	183	126
Panama	102	107	62
Paraguay	178	167	106
Peru	149	116	79
Philippines	138	154	117
Rwanda	136	—	164
Senegal	115	81	141
Sierra Leone	176	136	166
Uganda	127	177	153
Venezuela, R. B.	194	166	65
West Bank and Gaza	118	207	—

Source: World Bank Institute, Worldwide Governance Indicators, and World Bank data, 2009.
Note: — Not ranked.

Appendix C. The Illicit Enrichment Questionnaire

Background Information

Country name:
Contact information:

Legal Framework

1. Is ILLICIT ENRICHMENT a crime in your country? (For purposes of this study, illicit enrichment is the criminalization of a significant increase in the assets of a public official that he or she cannot reasonably explain in relation to his or her lawful income.)

   Yes ☐   No ☐

   If yes, please include the relevant law below.

   _____

   _____

   If no, is "illicit enrichment" incorporated in other legal instruments (tax code, administrative laws, forfeiture laws, ethics codes, etc.)? If so, please specify.

   _____

   _____

2. What evidence is needed to prove an illicit enrichment offense? What type of evidence is presented in court? (documents, testimony)

   _____

   _____

3. How does the burden of proof shift during an illicit enrichment prosecution?

_____

_____

4. What according to your country's jurisprudence is considered a defense to the illicit enrichment offense, that is, what is considered a "reasonable explanation" of the source of assets?

_____

_____

Application Data

For this section, if statistics are available and public, please provide us with the relevant data requested below. If not, please provide approximate numbers.

5. How many cases of illicit enrichment have been brought in your country since the law was enacted? How many, in average, are brought each year?

_____

_____

6. Of the illicit enrichment prosecutions sought, what percentage resulted in convictions?

_____

_____

International Cooperation

7. Have you filed requests for international mutual legal assistance in relation to illicit enrichment investigations/prosecutions?

    Yes ☐   No ☐

    If yes, have you encountered problems in obtaining said assistance? Please describe.

_____

_____

Asset Recovery

8. What assets are subject to recovery in relation to illicit enrichment proceedings?

9. Have you recovered any assets in relation to an illicit enrichment prosecution?

    Yes ☐   No ☐

    If yes, in how many instances and what quantities were recovered?

    _____

    _____

Challenges

10. What are the main challenges in investigating and prosecuting illicit enrichment cases in your country?

    _____

    _____

Bibliography

ADB (Asian Development Bank) and OECD (Organisation for Economic Co-operation and Development). 2006. *Denying Safe Haven to the Corrupt and the Proceeds of Corruption: Enhancing Asia-Pacific Cooperation on Mutual Legal Assistance, Extradition, and Return of the Proceeds of Corruption.* Papers presented at the fourth Master Training Seminar of the ADB/OECD Anti-Corruption Initiative for Asia and the Pacific. Manila: OECD.

———. 2007. *Mutual Legal Assistance, Extradition, and Recovery of Proceeds of Corruption in Asia and the Pacific Frameworks and Practices in 27 Asian and Pacific Jurisdictions: Thematic Review; Final Report.* Anti-Corruption Initiative for Asia and the Pacific. Tokyo: ADB. http://www.adb.org/Documents/Books/MLA-Extradition-Thematic-Report/MLA-Extradition-Thematic-Report.pdf.

Bacio-Terracino, Julio. 2008. "Corruption as a Violation of Human Rights." International Council on Human Rights Policy, Geneva, January. SSRN: http://ssrn.com/abstract=1107918.

Botha, Andre Eduan. 2009. "Net Worth Method as a Tool to Quantify Income during Investigation of Financial Crime." Research Paper, University of South Africa.

Brun, Jean-Pierre, Larissa Gray, Clive Scott, and Kevin Stephenson. 2011. *Asset Recovery Handbook: A Guide for Practitioners.* Washington, DC: World Bank, Stolen Asset Recovery Initiative.

Calderón Navarro, Nelly. 2006. "Fighting Corruption: The Peruvian Experience." *Journal of International Criminal Justice* 4 (3): 488–509.

De Luca, Javier Augusto, and Julio E. López Casariego. 2002. "Enriquecimiento patrimonial de funcionarios, su no justificación y problemas constitucionales." *Revista de Derecho Penal* 2: 117–50.

Derencinovic, Davor. 2010. "Criminalization of Illicit Enrichment." *Freedom from Fear Magazine,* May 17. http://www.freedomfromfearmagazine.org/index.php?option=com_content&view=article&id=177:criminalization-of-illegal-enrichment&catid=47:issue-4&Itemid=183.

de Speville, Bertrand. 1997. "Reversing the Onus of Proof: Is it Compatible with Respect for Human Rights Norms?" Paper presented at the eighth International Anti-Corruption Conference, Lima, September. http://www.8iacc.org/papers/despeville.html.

Diaz-Aranda, Enrique. 2008. "¿Previene el delito de enriquecimiento ilícito de la corrupción?" Biblioteca Jurídica Virtual del Instituto de Investigaciones Jurídicas, Universidad Nacional de México, Mexico, DF.

Due Process of Law Foundation. 2007. "Evaluation of Judicial Corruption in Central America and Panama and the Mechanisms to Combat It: Executive Summary and Regional Comparative Study." Due Process of Law Foundation, Washington, DC.

European Commission. 2010. *Report from the Commission to the European Parliament and the Council on Progress in Romania under the Cooperation and Verification Mechanism.* COM(2010) 401 final. Brussels: European Commission, July 20.

Godinho, Jorge A. F. 2007. "Do crime de 'riqueza injustificada' (Artigo 28o da Lei no. 11/2003, de 28 de Julho)." *Boletim da Faculdade de Direito da Universidade de Macau* 11 (24): 17–49.

———. 2009. "The AO Man Long Corruption and Money Laundering Case." *Freedom from Fear* 47 (4): 1–5. http://www.freedomfromfearmagazine.org/index.php?option=com_content&view=article&id=183:the-ao-man-long-corruption-and-money-laundering-case&catid=47:issue-4&Itemid=183.

Greenberg, Theodore, Larissa Gray, Delphine Schantz, Michael Latham, and Carolin Gardner. 2010. *Stolen Asset Recovery: Politically Exposed Persons; a Policy Paper on Strengthening Preventive Measures.* Washington, DC: World Bank, Stolen Asset Recovery Initiative.

Greenberg, Theodore, Linda Samuel, Wingate Grant, and Larissa Gray. 2009. *A Good Practices Guide to Non-Conviction-Based Forfeiture.* Washington, DC: World Bank, Stolen Asset Recovery Initiative.

Henning, P. J. 2001. "Public Corruption: A Comparative Analysis of International Corruption Conventions and United States Law." *Arizona Journal of International and Comparative Law* 18 (1): 793–866.

Inter-American Juridical Committee. 1999. *Annual Report of the Inter-American Juridical Committee to the General Assembly.* Rio de Janeiro: IAJC.

International Council on Human Rights Policy. 2010. *Integrating Human Rights in the Anti-Corruption Agenda: Challenges, Possibilities, and Opportunities.* Geneva: Transparency International. http://www.ichrp.org/files/reports/58/131breport.pdf.

Jayawickrama, Nihal, Jeremy Pope, and Oliver Stolpe. 2002. "Legal Provisions to Facilitate the Gathering of Evidence in Corruption Cases: Easing the Burden of Proof." *United Nations Forum on Crime and Society* 2 (1): 23–32.

Jorge, Guillermo. 2003. "Notes on Asset Recovery in the U.N. Convention against Corruption." American Bar Association, Chicago.

———. 2007. *The Romanian Legal Framework on Illicit Enrichment.* Chicago: American Bar Association, Central European and Eurasian Law Initiative (ABA/CEELI).

———. 2009. *Recuperación de activos de la corrupción.* Buenos Aires: Editores del Puerto s.r.l.

———. 2010. "Enriquecimiento ilícito: El silencio de la corte y las opciones del congreso." In *Jurisprudencia penal de la Corte Suprema de Justicia de la Nación,* ed. L. G. Pitlevnik. Buenos Aires: Hammurabi.

Kofele-Kale, Ndiva. 2000. "The Right to a Corruption-Free Society as an Individual and Collective Human Right: Elevating Official Corruption to a Crime under International Law." *The International Lawyer* 34 (1): 149–78.

———. 2006a. *The International Law of Responsibility for Economic Crimes: Holding State Officials Individually Liable for Acts of Fraudulent Enrichment.* Farnham, U.K.: Ashgate Publishing.

———. 2006b. "Presumed Guilty: Balancing Competing Rights and Interests in Combating Economic Crimes." *International Lawyer* 40 (4): 909–44.

Lee, R. S. K. 2000. "The Application of Hong Kong's Basic Law in Criminal Litigation." Unpublished paper submitted to the fourteenth International Conference of the International Society for the Return of Criminal Law in Sandton, South Africa.

Lifestyle Check. 2007. *A Handbook for Civil Society.* Quezon City: Transparency and Accountability Network. http://www.scribd.com/doc/4939870/Lifestyle-Check.

Loucaides, L. G. 2004. "Protection of the Right to Property in Occupied Territories." *International and Comparative Law Quarterly* 53 (July): 677–90.

Low, Lucinda A., Andrea K. Bjorklund, and Kathryn C. Atkinson. 1998. "The Inter-American Convention against Corruption: A Comparison with the United States Foreign Corrupt Practices Act." *Virginia Journal of International Law* 38 (Spring): 243–92.

McWalters, Ian. 2003. *Bribery and Corruption Law in Hong Kong.* Singapore: LexisNexis Butterworths, a Division of Reed Elsevier (Singapore).

OAS (Organization of American States). 2009a. *Mechanism for Follow-up on the Implementation of the Inter-American Convention against Corruption.* OEA/Ser. L SG/MESCIC/doc238/09rev.4. Report prepared for the fifteenth Meeting of the Committee of Experts, Washington, DC, September 14–18. OAS, Rio de Janeiro, September 18.

———. 2009b. "The Oriental Republic of Uruguay: Final Report (Adopted at the September 18, 2009 Plenary Session)." In *Mechanism for Follow-up on the Implementation of the Inter-American Convention against Corruption.* Report prepared for the fifteenth Meeting of the Committee of Experts, Washington, DC, September 14–18. OAS, Rio de Janeiro, September 18.

———. 2009c. "Republic of Argentina: Final Report (Adopted at the September 18, 2009 Plenary Session)." In *Mechanism for Follow-up on the Implementation of the Inter-American Convention against Corruption.* OEA/Ser. L SG/doc238/09rev.4. Report prepared for the fifteenth Meeting of the Committee of Experts, Washington, DC, September 14–18. OAS, Rio de Janeiro, September 18.

———. 2009d. "Republic of Paraguay: Final Report (Adopted at the September 18, 2009 Plenary Session)." In *Mechanism for Follow-up on the Implementation of the Inter-American Convention against Corruption.* Report prepared for the fifteenth Meeting of the Committee of Experts, Washington, DC, September 14–18. OAS, Rio de Janeiro, September 18.

———. 2010a. *Annual Report of the Inter-American Juridical Committee to the General Assembly.* OEA/SER.G CP/doc.4469/10. Rio de Janeiro: OAS, February.

———. 2010b. "Bolivarian Republic of Venezuela: Final Report (Adopted at the March 25, 2010 Plenary Session)." In *Mechanism for Follow-up on the Implementation of the Inter-American Convention against Corruption.* Report prepared for the sixteenth Meeting of the Committee of Experts, Washington, DC, March 22–25. OAS, Washington, DC, March 25.

———. 2010c. "Colombia: Final Report (Adopted at the March 25, 2010 Plenary Session)." In *Mechanism for Follow-up on the Implementation of the Inter-American Convention against Corruption.* Report prepared for the sixteenth Meeting of the Committee of Experts, Washington, DC, March 22–25. OAS, Washington, DC, March 25.

———. 2010d. "Ecuador: Final Report (Adopted at the March 25, 2010 Plenary Session)." In *Mechanism for Follow-up on the Implementation of the Inter-American Convention against Corruption.* Report prepared for the sixteenth Meeting of the Committee of Experts, Washington, DC, March 22–25. OAS, Washington, DC, March 25.

———. 2010e. "Mexico: Final Report (Adopted at the March 25, 2010 Plenary Session)." In *Mechanism for Follow-up on the Implementation of the Inter-American Convention against Corruption.* Report prepared for the sixteenth Meeting of the Committee of Experts, Washington, DC, March 22–25. OAS, Washington, DC, March 25.

———. 2010f. "Nicaragua: Final Report (Adopted at the September 16, 2010 Plenary Session)." In *Mechanism for Follow-up on the Implementation of the Inter-American Convention against Corruption.* Report prepared for the seventeenth Meeting of the Committee of Experts, Washington, DC, September 13–16. OAS, Washington, DC, September 16.

———. 2010g. "Panama: Final Report (Adopted at the September 16, 2010 Plenary Session)." In *Mechanism for Follow-up on the Implementation of the Inter-American Convention against Corruption.* Report prepared for the seventeenth Meeting of the Committee of Experts, Washington, DC, September 13–16. OAS, Washington, DC, September 16.

Okuyucu-Ergün, Güne. 2007. "Anti-Corruption Legislation in Turkish Law." *German Law Journal* 8 (9): 903–14.

Pereira, Julio. 2003. "O crime de riqueza injustificada e as garantias do processo penal." *Boletim do CCAC* 7 (September): 1.

Police Federation of Australia. 2009. "Police Support Unexplained Wealth Legislation." Press Release. Police Federation of Australia, Canberra. http://www.pfa.org.au/files/uploads/Press_Release_240609__2_.pdf.

Posadas, Alehandro. 2000. "Combating Corruption under International Law." *Duke Journal of Comparative and International Law* 10 (2): 345–415.

Rudnick, A. G. 1992. "Cleaning Up Money Laundering Prosecutions: Guidelines for Prosecution and Asset Forfeiture." *Criminal Justice* 7 (1): 2–6.

Schmid, Jean-Bernard. 2006. "Off the Beaten Track: Alternatives to Formal Cooperation." In *Denying Safe Haven to the Corrupt and the Proceeds of Corruption: Enhancing Asia-Pacific Cooperation on Mutual Legal Assistance, Extradition, and Return of the Proceeds of Corruption,* 25–28. Papers presented at the fourth Master Training Seminar of the ADB/OECD Anti-Corruption Initiative for Asia and the Pacific. Manila: OECD.

Schroth, Peter W. 2002. "American Law in a Time of Global Interdependence: U.S. National Reports to the XVITH International Congress of Comparative Law; Section V, the United States and the International Bribery Conventions." *American Journal of Comparative Law (Supplement)* 50 (Fall): 32–642.

Schroth, Peter W., and Ana Bostan. 2004. "International Constitutional and Anti-Corruption Measures in the European Union's Accession Negotiations: Romania in Comparative Perspective." *American Journal of Comparative Law* 52 (1): 625–711.

Shams, Heba. 2001. "The Fight against Extraterritorial Corruption and the Use of Money Laundering Control." *Law and Business Review of the Americas* 7 (1-2): 85–134.

Sherman, Tom. 2006. *Report on the Independent Review of the Operation of the Proceeds of Crime Act 2002 (Cth).* Attorney General's Department, Australian Government, Canberra, July. http://www.ag.gov.au/Publications/Pages/ReportontheIndependent-ReviewoftheOperationoftheProceedsofCrimeAct2002(Cth)July2006.aspx.

Snider, Thomas R., and Won Kidane. 2007. "Combating Corruption through International Law in Africa: A Comparative Analysis." *Cornell International Law Journal* 40 (691): 692–747.

Snow, Thomas. G. 2002. "The Investigation and Prosecution of White-Collar Crime: International Challenges and the Legal Tools Available to Address Them." *William and Mary Bill of Rights Journal (Symposium: Prosecuting White-Collar Crime)* 11 (1): 209–44.

StAR (Stolen Asset Recovery Initiative). 2012. *Public Office, Private Interests: Accountability through Income and Asset Disclosure, a Companion Volume to Income and Asset Disclosure; Case Study Illustrations.* Washington, DC: World Bank, Stolen Asset Recovery Initiative.

Stessens, Guy. 2004. *Money Laundering: A New International Law Enforcement Model.* Cambridge, U.K.: Cambridge University Press.

United Nations General Assembly. 2002a. "Report of the Ad Hoc Committee for the Negotiation of a Convention against Corruption on its First Session, Held in Vienna from 21 January to 1 February 2002." UN doc. A/AC.261/4. United Nations, Vienna.

———. 2002b. "Revised Draft United Nations Convention against Corruption." A/AC.261/3/Rev.1, second session of the Ad Hoc Committee on the Negotiation of a Convention against Corruption, Vienna, June 17–28.

United Nations Office of the High Commissioner for Human Rights. 1984. "General Comment No. 13: Equality before the Courts and the Right to a Fair and Public Hearing by an Independent Court Established by Law (Art. 14): 04/13/1984." United Nations, Geneva.

UNODC (United Nations Office on Drugs and Crime). 2006. *Legislative Guide for Implementation of the United Nations Convention against Corruption.* United Nations, Vienna.

———. 2010. "Travaux Préparatoires of the Negotiations for the Elaboration of the United Nations Convention against Corruption." United Nations, Vienna, November.

University of Minnesota Human Rights Library. n.d. "The Right to Fair Trial." *Human Rights in the Administration of Justice,* ch. 6. University of Minnesota. http://www1.umn.edu/humanrts/ monitoring/adminchap6.html.

U.S. Internal Revenue Service, Department of Treasury. 1994. *Financial Investigations: A Financial Approach to Detecting and Resolving Crimes; Instructor's Guide and Student Workbook.* EDS 385–747 209–220. Washington, DC: U.S. Government Printing Office.

van der Does de Willebois, Emile, Emily M. Halter, Robert A. Harrison, Ji Won Park, and J. C. Sharman. 2011. *The Puppet Masters; How the Corrupt Use Legal Structures to Hide Stolen Assets and What to Do about It.* Washington, DC: World Bank, Stolen Asset Recovery Initiative.

Washington College of Law. 2000. "The Experts Roundtable: A Hemispheric Approach to Combating Corruption." *American University International Law Review* 15 (2): 759–812.

Wilsher, Dan. 2006. "Inexplicable Wealth and Illicit Enrichment of Public Officials: A Model Draft That Respects Human Rights in Corruption Cases." *Crime, Law, and Social Change* 45 (1): 27–53.

Cases

European Court of Human Rights

James and Others v. United Kingdom, European Court of Human Rights (1986).

J. B. v. Switzerland, Application no. 31827/96 (2001).

John Murray v. the United Kingdom, Judgment of 8 February 1996, Reports 1996-I, p. 49, para. 45.

Minelli v. Switzerland, Application no. 62, Section 38 (1983).

Salabiaku v. France, Application no. 141-A, Section 28 (1988).

Hong Kong SAR, China

Attorney General v. Hui Kin Hong, Court of Appeals no. 52 of 1995.

Attorney General v. Lee Kwong-kut, AC 951 (1993), at 975.

India

Adh v. Republic of India, CRMC no. 2008 of 1998 (2000), INORHC 179 (23 March 2000).

Bhogilal Saran v. State of M.P., CRA 1060/2004 (2006), INMPHC 274 (11 November 2006).

K. Dhanalakshmi v. State, Crl.A.1158 of 2000 (2007), INTNHC 1990 (19 June 2007).

K. Ponnuswamy v. State of Tamil Nadu by Inspector of Police (2001), INSC 354 (31 July 2001).

Krishnanand Agnahatri v. State of M.P. (1977), 1 SCC 816.

Nallammal v. State Rep. by Inspector of Police (1999), INSC 251 (9 August 1999).

N. Ramakrishnaiah TR.LRS v. State of Andhra Pradesh (2008), INSC 1767 (17 October 2008).

Sajjan Singh v. the State of Punjab, 1964 AIR 464; 1964 SCR (4) 630.

Saran v. State of M.P., CRA 1060/2004 (2006), INMPHC 274 (11 November 2006).

State by Central Bureau of Investigation v. Shri S. Bangarappa (2000), INSC 578 (20 November 2000).

State of Maharashtra v. Pollonji Darabshaw Daruwalla, 1988 AIR 88; 1988 SCR (1) 906; 1987 SCC Supl. 379; JT 1987 (4) 363; 1987 SCALE (2) 1127.

United States

Coffin v. United States, 156 U.S. 432 (1895), at 453.

Exchange National Bank of Chicago v. Abramson, 295 F.Supp. 87 (D.C. Minn. 1969).

United States v. Alfonzo-Reyes, 384 F.Supp. 2d 523 (D.P.R. 2005).

United States v. Project on Government Oversight, 543 F.Supp. 2d 55 (D.D.C. 2008).

United States v. Saccoccia, 18 F.3d 795, 800 n. 6 (9th Cir. 1994).

Treaties and Conventions

African Union. African Union Convention on Preventing and Combating Corruption, 11 July 2003, 43 I.L.M. 5. http://www.africaunion.org/officialdocuments/treaties_%20 Conventions%20protocols/conventio%20protocols/convention%20on%20 combating%2Ocorruption.pdf.

Economic Community of West African States. Protocol on the Fight against Corruption, 22 December 2001. www.transparenciacdh.uchile.cl/media/documentacion/ archivos/ua_2.doc.

Organisation for Economic Co-operation and Development. OECD Convention on Combating Bribery of Foreign Public Officials in International Business Transactions, 17 December 1997, 1997 U.S.T. LEXIS 105. http://www.oecd.org/document/2 1/0,3.343,en_2649_34859_2017813_1_1_1_1,00.html.

Organization of American States. Inter-American Convention against Corruption, 29 March 1996, 1996 U.S.T. LEXIS 60, 35 I.L.M. 724. http://www.oas.org/juridico/ english)Treaties/b-58.html.

United Nations. Declaration against Corruption and Bribery in International Commercial Transactions, 16 December 1999, A/RES/51/191. http://www. un.org/documents/ ga/res/51/a51r191.htm.

United Nations. International Covenant on Civil and Political Rights, 23 March 1976, G.A.Res 2200A, U.N. Doc.A/6316. http://www.hrweb.org/legal/cpr.html.

United Nations. United Nations Convention against Corruption, G.A. Res. 58/4, U.N. Doc. A/58/422 (31 October 2003). http://www.unodc.org/pdf/crime/conventioncor-ruption/signing/convention-e.pdf.

United Nations. United Nations Convention against Illicit Traffic of Narcotic Drugs and Psychotropic Substances, Article 5, 20 December 1988, 1988 U.S.T LEXIS 194,28 I.L.M. 497. http://www.unodc.org/pdf/treaty adherenceconvention_1988.pdf.

United Nations. United Nations Convention against Transnational Organized Crime, 8 January 2001, G.A. Res. 55/25. U.N. Doc. A/RES/55/25. http://untreaty.un.org/english/treatyevent2003_1.htm.

United Nations. Universal Declaration of Human Rights, 10 December 1948, G.A.Res. 217A. http://www.un.org/Overview/rights.html.